Architecture of the Old South

MISSISSIPPI & ALABAMA

Architecture of the Old South

MISSISSIPPI & ALABAMA

MILLS LANE

Special Photography by VAN JONES MARTIN

Editorial Assistance by ROBERT GAMBLE,

MARY WARREN MILLER *and* RONALD W. MILLER

Drawings by GENE CARPENTER *and* DEBORAH LEWIS

A BEEHIVE PRESS BOOK

Abbeville Press · Publishers · New York

Frontispiece:
Longwood, Dr. Haller Nutt Villa,
Natchez, Mississippi, begun 1860.

Library of Congress Cataloging-in-Publication Data

Lane, Mills.
   Architecture of the Old South. Mississippi/Alabama / Mills
Lane; special photography by Van Jones Martin; drawings
by Gene Carpenter.
      p.   cm.
   Bibliography: p.
   Includes index.
   ISBN 1-55859-008-0
   1. Architecture—Mississippi.   2. Architecture, Colonial—
Mississippi.   3. Architecture, Modern—19th century—Mis-
sissippi.   4. Architecture—Alabama.   5. Architecture, Co-
lonial—Alabama.   6. Architecture, Modern—19th century—
Alabama.   I. Title.
NA730.M7L3   1989
720'.9761—dc19   89-6517
                                                  CIP

All photographs, unless otherwise credited, are by Van Jones
Martin.

Contents

Holly Springs

Florence · Athens
Town Creek · Huntsville
Tuscumbia · Courtland
Decatur
Moulton

Oxford

Pontotoc

Houlka

Aberdeen
Ashville · Jacksonville

Columbus
Talladega

French Camp

Lexington
Tuscaloosa

Foote
Eutaw
Gainesville · Greensboro
Forkland · Marion
Opelika

Mannsdale · Canton
Pocahontas · Madison · Prairieville
Vicksburg · Wetumpka
Clinton · Jackson · Demopolis · Uniontown · Prattville · Tuskegee
Raymond · Selma
Linden · Cahaba · Lowndesboro
Montgomery

Port Gibson · Union Springs

Rodney

Church Hill · Eufaula

Natchez

NATCHEZ TRACE

TOMBIGBEE RIVER

ALABAMA RIVER

Woodville

MISSISSIPPI
&
ALABAMA

Mobile

Biloxi

0 10 20 30 40 50

This volume continues a series of books about the historic buildings of the Old South. Each volume illustrates and describes the important and beautiful buildings—restored, unrestored, demolished and sometimes designs that were never executed—of one or two states, arranged in a sensible chronological and stylistic order and set in a brief cultural and social background. This fifth volume of the series is devoted to Mississippi and Alabama, the states carved from the historic Mississippi Territory. Just as every student, including this one, leans on the researches of others, this book is intended as a framework for further study. Because so many courthouses have burned and collections of family papers are so scarce in the Deep South, there is much more to learn about buildings in Mississippi and Alabama.

There have been many books about American architecture in general, but these general surveys too often illustrate the same famous buildings, select didactic examples and impose an artificial, if grand, orderliness on the subject. There have been few recent serious studies about the historic buildings of individual states. Many people know the most famous buildings of Mississippi and Alabama—Auburn at Natchez, the first house in the Mississippi Territory with a Classical portico; Gaineswood, the eccentric Greek Revival mansion in western Alabama; Waverley, another idiosyncratic Greek mansion outside Columbus, Mississippi; and Natchez's Longwood, the largest and most fabulous octagonal house in America. But even most experts are unfamiliar with Belle Mont, a Palladian mansion in northern Alabama; or Annandale, an Italianate villa in central Mississippi that was copied in detail from the last of Minard Lafever's pattern books; or nearby Ingleside, a sprawling Italian villa with colonnades leading to advanced dependencies; or the Chapel of the Cross at Mannsdale, Mississippi, whose Gothic design was inspired by a specific medieval church in England.

Buildings are three-dimensional history books that reflect the comings and goings, successes and failures of real people. Trickles of pioneers and Indian traders had begun making their way down the Ohio and Mississippi rivers in the 1790's and settled along the east bank of the lower Mississippi, and considerable numbers of Virginians, Kentuckians and Tennesseans filtered into northern Alabama just before and after the War of 1812. But substantial settlement of present-day Mississippi and Alabama was delayed by an international rivalry for control of the area and by Indians who continued to occupy the territory until the late 1830's. Considering the brief period of stability and wealth before the Civil War, it is surprising to find so much important architecture in the new states carved from the Mississippi Territory. These buildings were produced by a flood of energet-

Foreword

ic and talented entrepreneurs and settlers from the upper and seaboard South, New England, New York, Pennsylvania, Scotland and Ireland.

The Civil War marks the triumph of industrialization in America, homogenizing the nation's cultural life and beginning the end of regionalism in our country's architecture. But despite this series' title, *Architecture of the Old South*, buildings throughout America were probably more alike than they were different. The great architectural styles of early America—colonial Georgian, Adamesque Federal, the Greek Revival and the Gothic Revival—were all international movements. Professional architects from England and New York introduced the Greek Revival to Mississippi and Alabama. Most of the great buildings of the South were designed by professionals from outside the region or copied from builders' pattern books published at London, Boston, Philadelphia or New York. The first important builder in the Mississippi Territory was Levi Weeks, who came to Natchez from Massachusetts by way of New York. The young and gifted James Dakin and his brother Charles, who had worked for Ithiel Town and Alexander Jackson Davis in New York, came to the burgeoning Southwest in the 1830's and produced buildings at Mobile in the style of New York City. Other exciting Northern architects who worked in Mississippi and Alabama include Stephen Decatur Button, Samuel Sloan and John Stewart of Philadelphia. A cache of some sixty letters at the New York Public Library from Alabama planters to Richard Upjohn in New York illuminate the process of mail-order architecture in 19th-century America. A set of sixteen drawings by New York's Calvert Vaux, complete except for the plan of the first story, has survived for an Italian villa at Oxford, Mississippi, a treasure unique in the South. At least a dozen buildings in Mississippi were constructed with sawnwork ornament, columns and windows manufactured by Hinkle, Guild and Company of Cincinnati in the late 1850's. It seems evident that much of what some experts have described as Southern architecture is an accident of geography and exists mostly in the preconceptions of the beholder.

The most "Southern" buildings of the Old South are found in Mississippi and along the Gulf coast of Alabama, which endure the hottest, longest and most humid summers in the region, and in Louisiana, where the climate may be even harsher. Here the wide porches and galleries, long windows, open stairways and halls and raised basements were necessary accommodations to the severe climate. Mississippi and Alabama were substantially populated by Southerners from the upper and coastal states who had already learned how to adapt to climate. Somewhere in east-central Alabama there is an imaginary border that divides the older states of the upper and coastal South, with their more moderate climate and conservative building traditions, from the newer states of the lower South, with their harsher climate and freewheeling spirit.

Indeed, upon a close look at the architecture of one state, the forces of localism seem, paradoxically, to be stronger than regionalism. The Virginia tidewater had been settled two hundred years before Mississippi and Alabama. The rapid settlement of the Mississippi Territory produced a diversity rather than a similarity of building forms, types and styles. Groups of neighbors and relatives from one district in an older seaboard state often moved as a group to the frontier, and so the architecture of one community in Alabama might bear a closer resemblance to a town in North Carolina than to any other settlement elsewhere in Alabama. Natchez was strongly influenced by its trade with Cincinnati and St. Louis, Mobile by New York City, northern Alabama by Tennessee, and central Alabama by Georgia. The special cultural and economic factors shaping one prosperous community, one influential patron and his admirers or one talented craftsman and his apprentices or imitators often created clusters of distinctive buildings. A New Jersey-born builder named Jacob Larmour enjoyed the patronage of a rich widow in Canton, Mississippi. In Alabama, George Steele of Huntsville, Hiram Higgins of Athens and Benjamin Parsons, a New Englander transplanted to the black belt of Marengo County, produced groups of buildings with a discernible style.

We have already seen in previous volumes how Virginia had been the largest, richest and most populous English colony in the South, with early architecture of unsurpassed richness and variety. But by 1820, the population began to move from the old, exhausted tobacco lands of the upper and coastal South to the fertile new lands of the Mississippi River Valley. South Carolina was also a well-established and prosperous colony with important buildings. In the 1830's South Carolina also began to suffer a precipitous decline in growth and quality of architecture. North Carolina was an early colony, but, with treacherous coasts, poor harbors and shallow rivers, it was slow to develop. Georgia was the last and poorest colony, and less than a handful of pre-Revolutionary buildings have survived there. Georgia enjoyed its greatest prosperity during the heyday of the Greek Revival.

Now that our exploration of the South has moved into Mississippi and Alabama, we begin to appreciate the relationship between the history and buildings of the old, well-established coastal states, Virginia, Maryland, the Carolinas, and the rougher frontier states, Georgia, Alabama, Mississippi, Louisiana, Tennessee and Kentucky. In future volumes, we will learn more about the great variety of buildings throughout the region as well as about the South's contribution to American architecture in general.

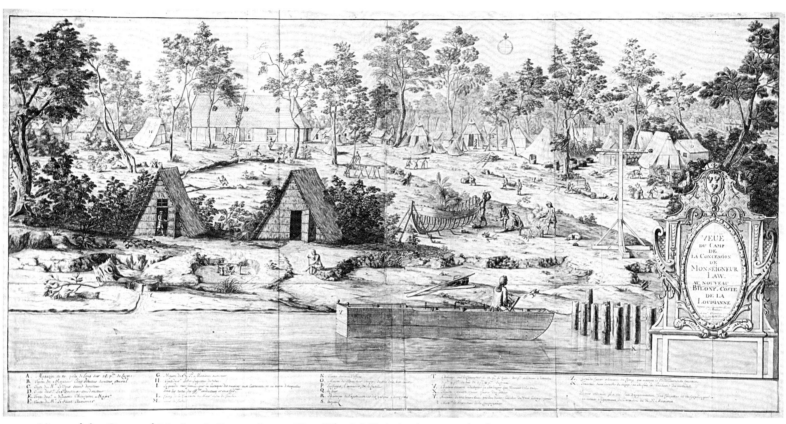

View of the Camp of Mr. Law's Concession at New Biloxi, Mississippi, watercolor by Jean-Baptiste Michel Le Bouteux, 1720. *Newberry Library, Chicago, E. E. Ayer Collection*

I. *Colony and Frontier*

French explorers from Canada ventured down the Mississippi River to the Gulf of Mexico at the end of the 17th century. In 1699 a fort was built on the northeast shore of Biloxi Bay, in present-day Mississippi. It was a rectangular wooden structure with corner bastions, armed with fourteen cannons. A new outpost was built on the other side of the bay at New Biloxi in 1720. Jean-Baptiste Michel Le Bouteux's evocative drawing of this camp pictures laborers at work and several varieties of early construction—tents, palmetto-thatched huts and timber-framed buildings.[1]

Other settlements were established at Mobile, near the Gulf, in 1711 and at Natchez, 150 miles up the Mississippi River, five years later. Professionally trained military engineers began building ambitious fortifications and public buildings. Adrien de Pauger, the chief military engineer of the French colony for three years before his death in 1726, presented elegant drawings for barracks and other buildings for Fort Condé at Mobile, derived from military books of the period. Mobile prospered under British rule in the 1760's and 1770's but languished under Spanish control between 1780 and 1813. When the Americans finally occupied the town in 1813, Mobile had only ninety wooden houses and 300 people.

Meanwhile, Natchez suffered near destruction by Indian attacks in the 1720's and was neglected until its occupation by the English in the 1760's and 1770's and by the Spanish in the 1780's and 1790's. In 1776 Natchez was still a village of ten log cabins and two frame buildings occupied by six or eight families, with some seventy other families living in the neighborhood. There was also an abandoned fort, a pentagonal stockade of five-inch-thick planks, enclosing a handful of timber-frame buildings, their walls insulated with mud and moss.[2]

Further substantial settlement of present-day Mississippi and Alabama, beyond the banks of the River and Gulf coast, was delayed for a century by an international dispute for control of the territory between France, Spain, Britain, Georgia, the government of the youthful United States and several Indian tribes. Natchez was ceded to the Americans by the Spanish

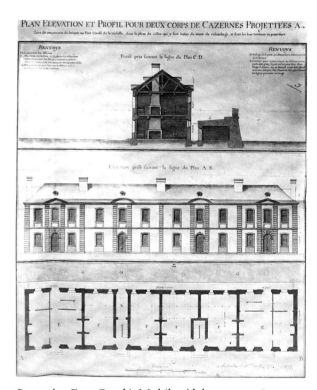

Barracks, Fort Condé, Mobile, Alabama, 1738.
Archives Nationales

in 1795. Seven years later, Georgia, which had attempted to sell lands in present-day Mississippi and Alabama to speculators, surrendered her Western claims. In 1811 the Americans seized Mobile and the Gulf coast. Two years later Andrew Jackson crushed the Creek Indians and captured their lands in southern Alabama. Meanwhile, the Creeks continued to claim most of central Alabama, while the Choctaws occupied the southern two-thirds of Mississippi and the Chickasaws occupied the upper third of Mississippi until the late 1830's. The final removal of these tribes in 1838 opened millions of acres of land and began an era of tremendous growth and speculation in Mississippi and Alabama.

In 1798, when the U.S. Congress created the Mississippi Territory, which included most of present-day Mississippi and Alabama except for a strip along the Gulf of Mexico, its population was some 4500 whites and 3500 blacks. Kentucky and Tennessee had been settled rapidly in the 1780's and 1790's, and by the turn of the century land-hungry settlers from the coastal states began to turn toward the fertile Southwest. Some of these settlers followed the Federal Road from Richmond by way of Raleigh, North Carolina, to Columbia, South Carolina, to Milledgeville, Georgia, to St. Stephens, an old fort and frontier outpost on the lower Tombigbee River above Mobile Bay. Other settlers journeyed down the Valley of Virginia through Knoxville and Nashville, Tennessee, settling along the Great Bend of the Tennessee River in northern Alabama or following the Natchez Trace, a 600-mile Indian path, to the banks of the lower Mississippi River. In 1817, James Graham of Hillsborough, North Carolina, wrote: "I have it in contemplation to explore the Mississippi State and Alabama Territory. . . . The Alabama Fever rages here and has carried off vast numbers of our citizens. . . . If it continues to spread it will almost depopulate the country!"[3] Mississippi was made a state in 1817, and Alabama, after only two years as a separate territory, became a state in 1819. The population of present-day Mississippi and Alabama swelled from 40,000 in 1810, to 200,000 in 1820, to 445,000 in 1830, to 965,000 in 1840, to 1,375,000 in 1850, to 1,660,000 in 1860.[4] By 1860, Mississippi and Alabama were producing more cotton than any other states in the Union, tremendous wealth that was reflected in rich new buildings.

The log cabin was the ubiquitous dwelling of the early American frontier. William Ely, a land agent from Connecticut who spent 1820–21 in Alabama, wrote home to New England: "I am weary with travelling over Mountains, thro Swamps & Mud & living in the middle of Piles of logs with no other Windows than the large spaces between them (there not being a Pane of Glass to 5,000 People in this Country). . . . Throughout this Country [there] are almost wholly miserable Log Cabins or Pens so open as not to require windows either for the purpose of lighting or ventilating them." From Tuscaloosa, Alabama, he wrote: "What they call their *houses* are either the most despicable rough, dirty & uncomfortable rolling log cabins or less durable & more mean buildings, most of them without a single Pane of Glass, with scarcely a saw'd board or Plank, Nail or any other Iron about them, all with Wooden Chimneys. . . . Some have no floor but the bare Earth, others have split flat pieces of Timber, or rough boards, laid either flat on the earth or on logs or poles lying on the Ground, without any fastening."[5]

Frontiersmen were not unskilled, but they were in a hurry. "O, my sister," lamented Sarah Fountain, who had just come from South Carolina to Dallas County, Alabama, in 1835, "I can't describe to you my feelings here in this strange country without house or home, so far separated from my dear friends!"[6] Colonial timber-frame construction used square timbers, fitted together in a complicated pattern with wooden pegs, a painstaking and slow process. Log buildings were made by laying logs horizontally, fitting them together at the corners with simple notched joints, so that each log was held in place by the weight of the log above it. The log cabin may have wasted wood, which was plentiful in the frontier, but it saved labor, which was scarce. In late 1818, after twenty years of restless wandering through South Carolina, Georgia, Alabama and Tennessee, a settler named Gideon Lincecum camped near a Choctaw settlement in northeast Mississippi. With the help of his brothers and a neighbor, he was able to raise the walls of his cabin on the first day, lay a floor of "linwood puncheons" on the second, make clapboards on the third, build a wooden chimney on the fourth and move into his new house on the fifth day.[7]

Because logs could not be arranged conveniently to form gable ends, a sawed frame and weatherboarding were used to build the upper parts of the walls. Often the walls were raised several extra feet above the ceiling joists before the gable roof was begun, allowing for greater headroom in the attic, which could be reached by a ladder from the ground story. Window openings, if any, were left unglazed, closed only by shutters. Gaps between the logs were filled by throwing clay violently into the cracks and then smoothing the surface. Rotting logs and eroding clay were always nagging problems, and settlers experimented with building wider eaves or covering the walls with plaster or weatherboards. John Looney's two-story cabin, built five miles north of Ashville, Alabama, about 1820 by an early settler from Tennessee, has been stripped of the original weatherboarding which probably covered its walls from an early date, to reveal the log construction. Looney House is open to the public. The naked logs give the visitor a misleading impression of the appearance of the exterior.

Captain Jonathan Cunningham Cabin, undocumented, Rogersville vicinity, Alabama. *Library of Congress*

Room sizes were limited to the available lengths of tree trunks that did not taper too greatly—usually about twenty feet—but log houses could be enlarged indefinitely by adding rooms or "pens" of stacked logs. Except for the one-room cabin, the most widespread house was made by building two log rooms and connecting them with a wide, open passageway. Samuel Forman, a settler who came down the Ohio and Mississippi rivers, later recalled his arrival at Natchez with his father in 1790: "The place had a small clearing and a log house on it, and he put up another log house to correspond with it, about fourteen feet apart, connecting them with boards, with a piazza in front of the whole. The usual term applied to such a structure was that it was 'two pens and a passage.' "[8] The open hall served as a sitting room and dining room. Because it also served as a kennel for the family dog, this house type is often called a dogtrot cabin. In 1836 Sarah Fountain, a settler from North Carolina, described her new home in Dallas County, Alabama: "It is a double house with a narrow passage between, the rooms are small and very open, there are cracks where the joists go in almost large enough for a dog to go through, but they answer for windows as we have no others. The loft is nothing but some loose boards laid down and [there is] no way to get up but to climb up the logs. . . . We have two beds in one room and three in the other. Consequently we have to set our door (for we have no table) in the passage . . . to eat off of. Pa and Samuel have made us four teaster bedsteads out of little saplins."[9]

Two years later, in 1838, Philip Gosse, an English naturalist who came to Dallas County as a plantation tutor, described a typical log house: "Very many of the houses . . . are built double; a set of rooms on each side of a wide passage, which is floored and ceiled in common with the rest of the house, but is entirely open at each end . . . forming a thoroughfare for the family through the house. . . . I will try to give you an idea of one about a mile distant. . . . It is a ground-floor house of two rooms. Fancy the walls full of crevices an inch or more in width, some of them running the whole length of the rooms caused by the warping of the logs, the decay of the bark, or the dropping out of the clay which had been put in to fill [them] up. There is no window in the whole house; in one room there is a square hole about two feet wide, which a shutter professes to close. . . . A door, rarely shut, gives light and air to each room. The lowest tier of logs composing the house rests on stout blocks about two feet from the ground, beams go across from these logs, on which the floor is laid; the planks are certainly sawed, but they are not pinned to the beams. . . . No ceiling meets the eye; the gaze goes up beyond the smoke-burnt rafters to the very shingles. . . . The chimney is merely a series of flat strips of wood, laid one upon another, in the form of a square, plastered within and without with well-beaten clay. It is, according to the average, a very decent house."[10]

Five years later, in 1843, Benjamin Smith moved into a log house built by his father in Lowndes County, Mississippi. In his old age, Smith described in unusual detail this "double log house, of large hewn logs, with ten-foot hall between, floored with rough plank. At each end of this hall was a small board shelter, which answered for a porch, resting on two peeled poles set in the ground. There were no floors to these shelters. The chimneys were of wood and the cracks in these as well as cracks in the house were filled with wood and daubed with mud in which hog hair was placed. The floors were of dressed matched timbers, with batten doors made of similar lumber. The rafters of this house were made of small round poles peeled and sheathing was of split laths, three inches wide and three-fourths of an inch thick, and covered with oak boards thirty inches long. The furniture consisted of one cheap plain bedstead, in each room, fastened together with cotton rope cords, and a trundle bed under my mother's bed, six unpainted plain split-bottom chairs, and a similar rocker . . . a cheap wardrobe, book case and table, the two latter made by a neighbor carpenter, also two small hanging mirrors."[11] Smith lived in his cabin for ten years, until 1853 when his father was able to build a more substantial frame house.

It was not only wild-eyed frontiersmen but thrifty and prosperous planters who lived in log cabins. Despite the moonlight and magnolia mythology that has obscured the plain reality of Southern life, the vast majority of farmers lived in modest comfort but without much display. Even rich farmers put their money in land and slaves, not in big houses, for they expected to migrate to new lands as soon as their fields had become worn out and unproductive. In 1835 the English traveller Harriet Martineau visited an Alabama planter who lived in "a log-house with the usual open passage in the middle" but had filled it with an "abundance of books and handsome furniture and plate." Miss Martineau's bedroom was well furnished, but she could "see the stars through the chinks between the logs."[12] In 1838 Philip Gosse was surprised to find that even the "wealthy and respectable planters" of Dallas County, Alabama, lived in cabins "of rough and unhewn logs." In 1842 Elizabeth Larabee of Rome, New York, travelling to Pontotoc, Mississippi, observed that "the richest man in all these parts" was living in "a long log house with two square rooms in front & a large square hall with immens[e] folding doors at both ends."[13] Though he lived in a log house, a rich farmer might fill it with mahogany furniture from the coast, a Brussels carpet from England, gilt mirrors and even a piano from New York. Cornelia Spencer described her neighbors of Clin-

Frame house with dogtrot plan, c. 1840, William Lowndes Yancey plantation, Montgomery County, Alabama, now moved to North Hull Street Historic District in Montgomery. *University of Alabama Library*

James Drane House, French Camp, Mississippi, 1846–48.

ton, Alabama, in 1858: "Most of the rich people who settled here when it was all new had to live in log houses. Now they are old and rich, they think the log houses will still do well enough with a little addition here and there. When a daughter comes home from boarding school, she will insist on a carpet for the parlour and a piano. . . . I was at a dinner at Col. M——'s. Well! Silver and china and cut glass and turkey and jelly and what-not on the table, and *such* holes in the wall of the house all around where the chinking had fallen from *between the logs* that I kept shaking like a dog all the time I was there!"[14] Log construction continued until long after the Civil War in remote parts of Mississippi and Alabama.

As forests and plank roads yielded to village life and railroads along this rapidly evolving frontier, frame construction gradually replaced logs, and by the mid-19th century the typical farmhouse was a two-story, gable-roofed building with exterior end chimneys, center hall, shed front porch and rear shed rooms. This type was most often built by settlers from Georgia and the Carolinas, where these "plantation-plain" houses are most commonly found. But the most distinctive feature of the plan of log houses—the wide open central passage—remained a feature of many frame buildings. William Yancey, the outspoken politician who came from Georgia to Alabama in the late 1830's, had a one-story frame house with an open center passage at his plantation in Coosa County. Howell Rose's two-story frame house, built in the early 1840's north of Wetumpka, Alabama, also features an open center passage on the first story. Both the Yancey and Rose houses have been moved to the Hull Street Historic District in Montgomery and are open to the public. James Drane, one of the first settlers of Choctaw County, Mississippi, who came from Georgia a decade earlier, built a two-story frame house with an open center passage in 1846–48. Like the house at Pontotoc, Mississippi, observed by Elizabeth Larabee in 1842, this open hall could be closed by pairs of wide folding doors. The Drane House, moved to a new site at French Camp, Mississippi, is open to the public.

Howell Rose House, c. 1840, Wetumpka, Alabama, vicinity, now moved to North Hull Street Historic District in Montgomery.

II. *The Federal Era*

An early 19th-century view of Natchez, Mississippi, lithograph by Ed. de Montule. *Historic Natchez Foundation*

Spanish jail, Natchez, Mississippi, drawing by William Dunbar, 1798. *Archivo General de Simancas*

In the 1790's, Natchez was a village of some eighty-five houses. The largest of these was built for the Spanish governor, Manuel Gayoso de Lemos. The Tuscan columns, pedimented portico and pair of curving front steps were not added to Governor Gayoso's house until the 1820's or 1830's for a later owner. This house burned in 1901. Like many Gulf coast–Mississippi River houses of the era, it was a large frame cottage raised on a tall brick basement and surrounded by wide galleries. In plan, these houses were typically wider than they were deep, often merely consisting of a single file of rooms to facilitate cross ventilation. The galleries shaded the exterior walls and also took the place of interior hallways, so stairs were located on the open galleries and not inside the house. The earliest surviving examples date from the period of Spanish rule in the 1790's. Scholars have found parallels in France and the West Indies and as far north as Illinois. But it is not yet clear whether these galleried houses reflect persistent French influence, brought by early colonists from Europe and traders from the West Indies, or represent a spontaneous and widespread attempt to protect the walls and windows of buildings from sun and rain in this torrid climate. William Dunbar's 1798 drawing of a jail at Natchez illustrates a two-story frame building with a gable roof, a wide building only one room deep, surrounded by shed-roofed galleries. The merchant James Moore built a house like this about 1791 on one of the hillsides overlooking the river at Natchez.

In the 1790's, Americans began to flock to the banks of the lower Mississippi River, many of them New Englanders who travelled a thousand miles from the Ohio River toward the Gulf of Mexico. The first brick building, a tavern that was later used as a meeting place for the state legislature, was built for a Spanish-born merchant named Manuel Texada about 1799. In 1801 Peter Little, still in his early twenties, moved to Natchez from Pennsylvania and established a sawmill propelled by the first steam engine brought into the Mississippi Territory. Three years later, George Hunter reported from Natchez: "Every thing here is very dear,

Concord, Manuel Gayoso de Lemos House, Natchez, Mississippi, c. 1795, portico and stairs added c. 1830. *Private Collection*

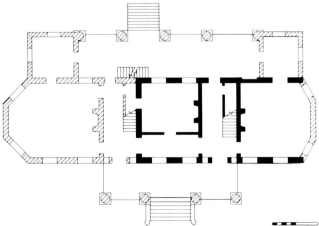

Gloucester, Samuel Young House, Natchez, Mississippi, c. 1803, enlarged for Winthrop
Sargent 1807, portico added c. 1830. Plan of the principal story indicates additions to
the original house.

rents very high & Mechanicks very scarce."[1] In October, 1812, a new-comer from Massachusetts wrote of Natchez: "The houses are extremely irregular and for the most part temporary things—but of late a number of good houses have been built."[2] At this time there were six carpenters, three house painters, four master bricklayers and two plasterers in the town. By 1820 Natchez had become a city of some 150 houses, with an area population of 2200 people, the largest and wealthiest town between New Orleans and St. Louis.

In 1798 Winthrop Sargent, appointed the first governor of the Mississippi Territory by President Adams, reached Natchez. Born in Massachusetts and educated at Harvard College, Sargent was one of the many newcomers from New England who contributed so much to the social and cultural development of the Old South. After his brief tenure as governor had ended, Sargent decided to remain in Mississippi. Purchasing a two-story, hip-roofed brick house that had been built about 1803 for Samuel Young, Sargent soon decided to improve it. In 1807 Henry Hunt, Sargent's plantation manager, wrote his employer that his friend Lyman Harding had suggested how to enlarge the house: "B. L. Harding has suggested the plan of building a wing to the house the same size to form an ell, from the east end to be built in uniformity with the other part."[3] Although Hunt had hired a brickmason, he had been unable to locate someone to make drawings. Sargent's house, which he called "Gloster" Place, features walls laid in Flemish bond (long sides and short ends of the bricks alternating in every course) and elaborate fanlight entrances set in carved frontispieces flanked by detached sidelights. The two-story Tuscan portico, with a bull's-eye window set in the pediment, was not added until the 1820's or 1830's. Springfield, another early house of related design, is located near the Natchez Trace some twenty miles north of Natchez. Springfield was built for Thomas Green, Jr., descended from Virginia settlers, about 1806–7 by a Kentuckian named John Hall. Springfield, like Gloucester, attempts grandeur with its careful brickwork, detached sidelights, delicate interior trim and a massive but ungainly two-story Tuscan portico, which was probably added in the 1830's.

The Mississippi Territory—at least a tiny part of it, the Natchez District—could now afford the pretensions of academic architecture. Despite the young nation's protestations of independence, American builders continued the traditions of English architecture in the post-Revolutionary era. In the mid-18th century English builders had copied the monumental forms of ancient public buildings as published in the works of the late Renaissance architect Andrea Palladio and his English popularizers, enriched in the last decades of the century by an intricate delicacy that reflected a rediscovered knowledge of ancient domestic architecture. The craftsmen who came to Natchez from the East, particularly from New England, brought with them knowledge of Roman porticoes, Tuscan columns, fanlights, and Palladian windows, cascading spiral stairs and swirling patterns of surface decoration, which is known in America as the Federal style. In the remote, rural South, hundreds of miles from the cosmopolitan ports of the East coast, these grand concepts were simplified by the limited knowledge and resources available to builders in the Mississippi Territory.

A grisly murder in New York City precipitated the introduction of Classical architecture to the Mississippi Territory. Levi Weeks, a carver and master builder from New England, came to Natchez about 1809, opened a cabinet and chair shop and established himself as a builder.[4] Born at Greenwich, Massachusetts, in 1776, Weeks had worked in New York City between 1798 and 1803 for his older brother Ezra, who was also a housewright. But Levi was accused of murdering his lover, Juliana Sands, and throwing her battered body down a well. Though he was finally acquitted, Levi's career in New York had been brought to an abrupt conclusion. After returning to Massachusetts for two years and then drifting from Cincinnati to Lexington, Kentucky, Weeks finally settled in the Mississippi Territory.

During his first three years at Natchez, Weeks built the Natchez Hospital, a three-story brick building intended for the care of sailors and paupers, an office for the Bank of Mississippi and a Presbyterian Church, all of which have been demolished. In 1812 Weeks was engaged in building a two-story brick mansion, Auburn, for Winthrop Sargent's friend Lyman Harding, a Massachusetts-born lawyer, also a director of the Bank of Mississippi and a commissioner of the Presbyterian Church, who had suggested the plan for enlarging Sargent's house, Gloucester. Writing to Epaphras Hoyt, a surveyor, postmaster and justice of the peace at Deerfield, Massachusetts, Weeks predicted that Harding's house, with its two-story Roman Ionic portico and Corinthian entablature, would be "the most magnificent Building in the territory . . . the first house in the Territory on which was ever attempted the orders of Architecture."[5] By "orders" Weeks meant the correct details of capitals, columns and entablatures of ancient Roman public buildings. Weeks's design was daring as well as magnificent, for it was the first monumental portico west of South Carolina.

Like most carpenters and builders in early America, Weeks copied these sophisticated designs from books. Auburn's portico is based on Abraham Swan's *Collection of Designs in Architecture* (London, 1757) with the

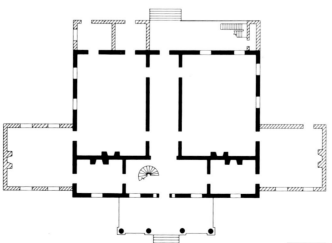

Auburn, Lyman Harding House, Natchez, Mississippi, 1812, wings added c. 1830. Plan indicates additions.

Auburn, entrance.

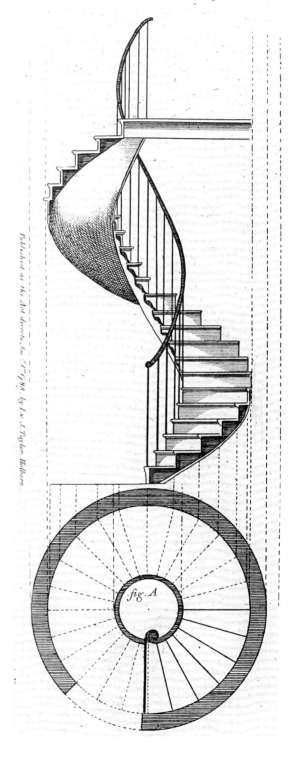

Auburn, "Geometrical staircase" in front hall, with its model, Plate 41 of William Pain's *British Palladio* (London, 1757). *Pain illustration from Art & Architecture Collection, Miriam & Ira D. Wallach Division of Art, Prints and Photographs, The New York Public Library, Astor, Lenox and Tilden Foundations*

Auburn, parlor doorway

capitals taken from William Pain's *British Palladio* (London, 1786). The distinctive reeded decoration surrounding the fanlight above the entrance, inspired by Roman fasces, the ceremonial bundles of rods carried by government officials, was suggested by a detail in Pain's Plate XXIII. Inside, the design of the "Geometrical staircase" in the entrance hall is derived from Plate 41 of Pain's book, and broken pediments over interior door-ways are copied from Plate 26 of William Salmon's *Palladio Londinensis* (London, 1734) and from pages 45 and 47 of Pain's *Builder's Companion* (London, 1758). These books reflected the taste of mid-18th-century England—in fact, the same design from *Palladio Londinensis* had been copied for a doorway at Westover on the James River of Virginia in the 1730's, ninety years earlier!—and explain why, despite their novelty in the Mississippi Territory, some of the details at Auburn appeared old-fashioned even when they were new. The wings and rear gallery of Auburn were added some time after 1827 for a later owner, Stephen Duncan, a Pennsylvania-born planter-physician who became one of the South's largest slaveowners, with a force of more than one thousand bondsmen. Auburn is open to the public.

In 1817 Weeks was employed in building the East wing of Jefferson College at Washington, a few miles north of Natchez, and the next year he was working as inspector of the boat landing at Natchez. When he died of yellow fever in 1819, Weeks's estate included a chest of tools, two drawing boards, two boxes of drawings, two T-squares, a bundle of drawing paper and a large collection of architecture books, which included Thomas Malton's *Complete Treatise on Perspective* (London, 1776), William Halfpenny's *Art of Sound Building* (London, 1728), William Pain's *British Palladio* (London, 1786), Abraham Swan's *Designs in Carpentry* (London, 1759), Swan's *Collection of Designs in Architecture* (London, 1757), Halfpenny's *The Modern Builder's Assistant* (London, 1742), Isaac Ware's edition of Palladio's *Four Books of Architecture* (London, 1738), the anonymous *Designs for Chimney-pieces* (London, 1793) and two American books, Owen Biddle's *Young Carpenter's Assistant* (Philadelphia, 1805) and Robert Gibson's *Treatise on Practical Surveying* (Philadelphia, 1789), plus an unidentified volume of "Designs for Architects Cabinetmakers." As Asher Benjamin, the Massachusetts carpenter and architectural author, wrote in 1806: "Old-fashioned workmen, who have for many years followed the footsteps of Palladio and Langley, will no doubt leave their old path with great reluctance."

The house at The Forest plantation was built in 1816, twelve miles south of Natchez, for the widow Dianah Dunbar. Her husband, William Dunbar, was a Scottish-born Indian trader and cotton planter. One of the most

The model for parlor doorway at Auburn, Plate 26 of William Salmon's *Palladio Londinensis* (London, 1734). *Virginia Historical Society*

Jefferson College, Washington, Mississippi. The East Wing, on the right, was built by Levi Weeks in 1817. The West Wing, on the left, was built in 1837. *Private Collection*

intriguing personalities in the Territory, he was a scientific farmer, amateur astronomer, meteorologist, linguist and correspondent of Jefferson, who nominated him to become a member of the prestigious American Philosophical Society at Philadelphia. Six years after Dunbar's death, his widow began construction of her new house. Though it burned in 1852, this mansion is known from an early drawing and the carpenter's original estimate. The mansion was a two-story hip-roofed structure, with a dentil or modillion eaves cornice, galleries with monumental Roman "dorick" or Tuscan columns, a frontispiece with leaded fanlight, sidelights and engaged columns or pilasters. Inside, there was a "ramp twist and wide stair case on an octigan [sic] plan."[6]

Joseph Holt Ingraham, a Yankee schoolteacher who came to the Natchez area about 1830, described a more typical plantation house of the early 19th century: "The dwelling, like most in Mississippi, was a long, wooden, cottage-like edifice, with a long piazza . . . extending along the front and rear of the building. This gallery is in all country-houses, in the summer, the lounging room, reception room, promenade and dining room." When Ingraham arrived, he found the planter sitting on his gallery, feet propped upon the railing, a nephew, fanned by a slave, asleep in a hammock, a litter of pups sleeping in a blanket, and the columns and walls cluttered with deer antlers, broad-brimmed hats, bridles, a riding whip, coat, spurs, shot-pouches, game-bags and a gun.[7] One of these cottages, typical in form but extraordinary in its careful detail, is The Briars, built about 1818 for John Perkins, a Maryland-born planter, on the bluff southwest of Natchez overlooking the Mississippi River. Sometimes porches were finished as if they were three-sided rooms, with a chairrail, panelled wainscot, plaster cornices and doorways at the porch ends. The Briars is embellished with slender Roman Doric colonnettes in place of the chamferred pillars that would have been favored earlier, and dormer windows with interweaving mullions and semicircular and elliptical fanlights.

Another house that is ordinary in form but extraordinary in detail is the two-story gable-roofed frame house built about 1816 for Thomas Reed, a settler from Kentucky who became one of Mississippi's first U.S. senators. Originally called Reedland but now known as Linden, Reed's house features elliptical fanlights and a refined two-tiered pedimented Tuscan portico. Wings and one-story extensions of the portico were added in the 1830's or 1840's for a later owner.

Builders were always copying each other, and now the wealthy merchants and planters of Natchez, the most prosperous and populous district anywhere in Mississippi and Alabama, began to demand brick mansions with monumental Tuscan or Roman Doric porticoes. Arlington was built

The Forest, Dianah Dunbar House, Natchez, Mississippi, vicinity, a 19th-century drawing. *Mississippi Department of Archives and History*

The Briars, John Perkins House, Natchez, Mississippi, c. 1818.

Linden, Thomas Reed House, Natchez, Mississippi, c. 1816, enlarged c. 1840.

for Hampton White about 1819–20. Its sumptuous details include marble window and door sills and lintels, an expansive semicircular fanlight and entablatures surmounting interior doorways. The rear porch was added in the 1830's and a cast-iron side porch was added in the 1850's. Rosalie, built in 1822–23 for the Pennsylvania-born sawmill owner Peter Little, features a Tuscan portico and a plan similar to Arlington's, with the stair set in a lateral passage. The interior of Rosalie was remodelled in the late 1850's. Rosalie is open to the public. Less is known of Clifton, another large brick mansion with a two-story portico, built on the bluff overlooking the river for Samuel Postlethwaite before 1825. Thomas Kilby Smith, a Union officer who came to Natchez in 1863, described Clifton as "one of the largest & most elegantly appointed mansions in all the South" and then demolished it to make way for Civil War fortifications.[8]

Andrew Brown, born in Scotland in 1793, was a builder and sawmill owner who came to Natchez by way of Pittsburgh about 1820. He built a lighthouse on the bluff of the river near town in 1827. Brown's other early work remains undocumented, but he is believed to have built the remarkable Masonic Hall of 1827. Demolished in 1890, the Masonic Hall had an elliptical entrance flanked by narrow pointed sidelights, engaged Corinthian columns and pilasters, an elaborate cornice and a projecting center pavilion with an oval window in the pediment. In the absence of documentation, we may also conjecture that Brown built the First Presbyterian Church at 117 South Pearl Street in 1828–29. The brick walls of the First Presbyterian Church were originally unstuccoed, so that the bright red brick contrasted vividly with the buff-color stuccoed pilasters. The walls were stuccoed in 1836, and the building was enlarged by James Hardie in 1851. The interior has been altered several times, most considerably in 1838 and 1859. Andrew Brown also drew the plans for a theater in 1826–27, a two-story brick building with fanlight entrances and a tier of boxes. The front elevation of the theater was drawn by a builder named John McCleary. At the end of his career, Andrew Brown supplied lumber for Longwood, the fabulous octagonal villa of the planter Haller Nutt, who paid tribute to Brown as "a very practical man and one of keen observation."

Rodney, located some twenty miles north of Natchez, is now a ghost town, but it was once a prosperous port of one thousand people, with two banks, two newspapers, a hotel, theater, two churches and a sawmill operated by the Weldon brothers. The Mississippi River shifted its channel several miles further west in the late 19th century and left the town's future, literally, high and dry. The elegant little Presbyterian Church, overlooking the nearly deserted street that was once so bustling, recalls Rodney's lost

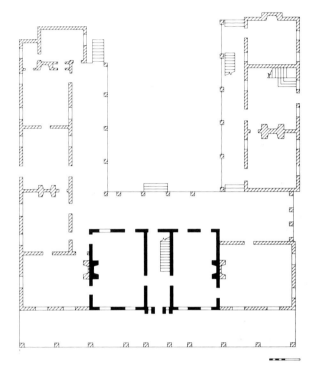

Plan of Linden, indicating additions.

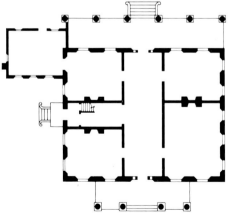

Arlington, Hampton White House, Natchez, Mississippi, c. 1819–20, with its plan.

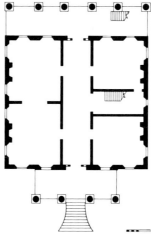

Rosalie, Peter Little House, Natchez, Mississippi, 1822–23, with its plan.

Masonic Hall, Natchez, Mississippi, 1827. *Private Collection*

glory. Though its interior has been gutted, the exterior features Flemish-bond walls, a curvilinear front gable, semicircular windows, elliptical fan-lights and an octagonal belfry. The name of its designer is unknown.[9]

Meanwhile, another area of early settlement had been established at the other end of the Natchez Trace. Kentucky and Tennessee had been settled rapidly in the 1790's. By the turn of the century a wave of immigration spilled over into the Tennessee River Valley and down to the Great Bend of the Tennessee River in the northwest part of present-day Alabama. By 1805 a settlement was flourishing on a bluff overlooking a spring at the foot of the Cumberland Mountains. When the first official land sales were held in 1809, the population of the Huntsville area was already 2223 whites and 322 slaves. The first court was held in 1810, the first newspaper was published in 1812, and a bank opened in 1816. Two years later Anne Royall from Maryland wrote of Huntsville: "It contains about 260 houses, principally built of bricks; has a bank, a courthouse, and market house. . . . Several of the houses are three stories high, and very large."[10] In April, 1823, Lucius Bierce, after travelling some 300 miles across the Southern frontier, reached Huntsville and there saw brick buildings for the first time since leaving Virginia.[11]

The largest group of trained builders working in northern Alabama came from Tennessee and Virginia.[12] The two earliest identified builders in Huntsville, the Virginia-born brothers Thomas and William Brandon, reached northern Alabama by way of Tennessee about 1810. As late as 1850, when the census recorded the birthplace of citizens for the first time, there were sixty-four carpenters working in Madison County (Huntsville). Of these, sixteen came from Tennessee, fifteen from Virginia, eleven from North Carolina, eight from South Carolina, seven were native born, with one each from Massachusetts, Connecticut, Kentucky, Ireland, Germany, Mississippi and Georgia.

Leroy Pope, a young Virginian who came to Alabama by way of Georgia in 1809, became the principal owner of the land on which the town of Huntsville was being built. His two-story, hip-roofed brick mansion, built in 1814 and enlarged about 1830, is the earliest surviving large-scale building in northern Alabama. Another fine house from this period was built in 1819 for Henry C. Bradford, a merchant from Tennessee, featuring an expansive semicircular fanlight. In the 1820's this house was the home of John McKinley, who came from Virginia by way of Kentucky and Tennessee and became a U.S. Senator and Supreme Court Justice. Between 1845 and 1956, the house was occupied by members of the Weeden family.[13] Weeden House is open to the public, in the center of a restored and revitalized historic district.

Presbyterian Church, Rodney, Mississippi, c. 1830.

Though the constitutional convention met at Huntsville to form a state government in July, 1819, the first permanent capitol of Alabama was built at Cahaba on the Alabama River in 1819–20, some twelve miles south of present-day Selma.[14] The builders were David and Nicholas Crocheron, members of a French family who had come to Alabama from Staten Island, New York. The State House at Cahaba was a two-story brick structure, fifty-eight feet long and forty-three feet wide, with a hipped roof. This State House was first occupied by the legislature when it met in November, 1820. Abandoned by the state government after only five years, this building served as a county courthouse until its demolition about 1835.

Another economic and social center of northern Alabama in the 1820's was Florence, located on a bluff overlooking the Tennessee River near Muscle Shoals. The town had been laid out in 1818 for a speculative land company by an Italian surveyor named Ferdinand Sonona. Within four years some one hundred dwellings, a cluster of warehouses, a courthouse and two taverns had been built. The builder of the courthouse, a two-story brick structure with a steeple, was a carpenter named Nathan Vaught from Maury County, Tennessee. As late as 1850, of the eighty-seven carpenters in Lauderdale County (Florence), twenty-five came from Tennessee, fifteen from Virginia, thirteen from North Carolina, twelve from South Carolina, ten were native born and others came from Georgia, Kentucky, Ireland and New York. The courthouse was demolished about 1900.

The industrious and well-educated Scotch-Irish settlers of Florence cultivated a taste for fine architecture. George Coulter, a lawyer who came to Alabama from Kentucky by way of Tennessee, purchased a lot on one of the highest hills overlooking the Tennessee River in the original land sale of 1818. Within about ten years he was able to afford the cost of a substantial residence. This house, now called Mapleton, is a two-story, gable-roofed frame building. The original portico, which was probably supported by two tiers of slender Tuscan columns (much like those at the 1816 Linden at Natchez), was replaced with heavy square pillars in the 1940's. The interior, with its panelled wainscot, carved pinwheels, swags, urns, grapes, pineapples and sunbursts, and a great elliptical arch springing from fluted consoles in the hall, is the finest that has survived from early Alabama.

Many Virginians made their way to northern and central Alabama by way of Tennessee and Kentucky. Though they were not the most numerous settlers, the Virginians, because of their wealth, education and prominence, made contributions to Alabama's early architecture far greater than their numbers. In 1834 Henry Watson, a New England lawyer, wrote from Greensboro, Alabama: "The country about is now settled by emigrants

Mapleton, George Coulter House, 420 South Pine Street, Florence, Alabama, c. 1830, portico replaced c. 1940.

Mapleton, view of hall from rear.

Woodlawn, James Hood House, Florence, Alabama, vicinity, 1830–32.

James Irvine House, 461 North Pine Street, Florence, Alabama, c. 1835.

from Virginia and the Carolinas . . . some of the nobility of the old states . . . the Randolph family, the Meades, the Tayloes, the Bollings, &c. The country is thus filled with much more intelligence than you would have expected."[15] Nathaniel Harrison Marks, a brickmason from eastern Virginia, built Woodlawn, originally called Woodland, in 1830–32, near Florence for the Irish-born planter-merchant James Hood. Woodlawn features semicircular leaded fanlights and one-story wings. James Sample, a storekeeper who came to the county from Pennsylvania in 1818, was the original owner of Wakefield, at 450 North Court Street, built in the mid-1830's. Another handsome brick house was built in the 1830's for James Irvine, an Irish-born lawyer, at 461 North Pine Street. The refined brickwork and stepped gables of the Sample and Irvine houses suggest the work of craftsmen from middle Tennessee, the transient home of many Virginians.

Many of Virginia's finest late-18th-century buildings had been inspired by the works of Andrea Palladio, the Renaissance Italian architect who had used columns, pediments or projecting pavilions to suggest the giant porticoes of ancient Roman temples, as well as raised first stories, balanced wings or flankers. Between about 1780 and 1820, Palladian traditions influenced the building of a group of smaller farmhouses in Virginia and the nearby counties of North Carolina, each with a two-story central block, a gable facing forward to form a temple-like pediment, and flanking one-story wings. This design, a diminutive palace, afforded grandeur on a modest scale and provided extra ventilation and natural light in each of the principal rooms.

Two outstanding houses of this type were built in northern Alabama for genteel Virginians who came down the Shenandoah Valley to the lower South in the 1820's. Belle Mont was built five miles south of Tuscumbia for planter-physician Alexander Mitchell, from Louisa County, Virginia, about 1828–32, on a commanding hilltop overlooking the low-lying cotton fields of his 1680-acre plantation. The elegant proportions and careful brickwork must have been produced by accomplished craftsmen from Virginia. The inventive U-shaped plan of Belle Mont, with wings forming a rear court, allows maximum ventilation through rooms in the torrid summer and maximum accumulation of warmth during winter. Belle Mont has been restored by the State of Alabama.

Saunders Hall, two miles north of the hamlet of Town Creek, was built about 1830–35 for a planter-merchant from Virginia, Turner Saunders. The two-story Tuscan portico carries a complete entablature with triglyphs and metopes and is flanked by one-story wings with surprising pediments and brick pilasters. A more remote and simpler example of a Palladian-

Palladian houses illustrated in William Halfpenny's *Useful Architecture* (London, 1752) and Robert Morris's *Select Architecture* (London, 1757). *Avery Architectural and Fine Arts Library, Columbia University*

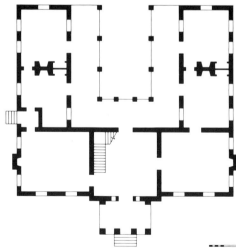

Belle Mont, Alexander Mitchell House, Tuscumbia, Alabama, vicinity, c. 1828–32, with its plan.

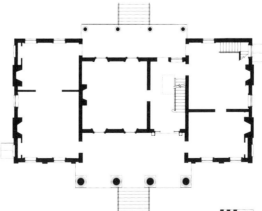

Saunders Hall, Turner Saunders House, Town Creek, Alabama, vicinity, c. 1830–35, with its plan.

Saunders Hall, entrance. *Photograph by Frances Benjamin Johnston, Library of Congress*

inspired farmhouse was built in Lafayette County, Mississippi, outside Oxford, about 1838 for Washington Price, a land speculator and mill owner from Wake County, North Carolina. He came to Mississippi with a group of skilled craftsmen who repeated the building formulas they had learned in North Carolina.

Palladianism was also brought firsthand to Alabama by a professionally trained architect from England. In 1825 the Alabama legislature moved the capital from low-lying, fever-infested Cahaba to Tuscaloosa, on the bluff of the Black Warrior River. Two years later, in 1827, William Nichols was employed as State Architect of Alabama to design and superintend construction of public buildings. Nichols was born in 1777 at Bath, the English city crowded with sumptuous late-18th-century villas and terraces, and sailed to North Carolina in 1800. Nichols was described in 1806 as "a Clerk, Draftsman, Surveyor, Architect and regular bred Workman, of considerable talents, ingenuity and merit." After working privately in New Bern, Edenton and Fayetteville, North Carolina, Nichols was appointed State Architect and remodelled the old State House at Raleigh in 1820–24. This work probably brought him to the attention of the authorities in Alabama. Then, like so many other North Carolinians, Nichols sought opportunity in the expanding Southwest.

Upon his arrival in Tuscaloosa in 1827, Nichols rejected a plan for the new Capitol that had been proposed by a legislative committee, a clumsy building described by one contemporary as having "more the appearance of a Dutch barn or a cotton factory than a state capitol," and substituted plans of his own.[16] The design that Nichols presented in December, like his remodelling of the North Carolina State House, included a cruciform plan, a projecting central pavilion with engaged Ionic columns, a rusticated ground story and a rotunda surmounted by a dome. Most exterior details of the Capitol were Roman—the building looked like a mid-18th-century English Palladian country house—but the State House also featured several specifically Greek details—small one-story Doric porticoes, doorways copied from the Temple of Theseus at Athens, a Greek fret in the rotunda, and a screen of columns in the Supreme Court copied from the Temple of the Winds.[17] Nichols brought some artisans from North Carolina, among them John Robb who carved the Ionic and Doric capitals, but Nichols also advertised in the newspapers of Cincinnati and other cities for additional craftsmen. The curving staircases at the Capitol were built by John Fitch, a carpenter from Massachusetts. First used by the legislature in November, 1829, and finally declared complete in 1831, the Capitol was abandoned by the state in the 1840's and was used as a school until it burned in 1923.

In March, 1828, Nichols presented plans for the University of Alabama,

Washington Price House, Oxford, Mississippi, vicinity, c. 1838, restored elevation.

Alabama State Capitol, Tuscaloosa, Alabama, 1827–31. *University of Alabama Library*

which was to be built north of Tuscaloosa facing the stage road to Huntsville. The architect envisaged a large quadrangle of brick buildings, dormitories, two professors' houses and a temple-like Lyceum, surrounding a domed Rotunda. The Lyceum was a two-story brick structure, with a raised basement and Ionic portico, containing classrooms. Each professors' house would provide lodgings for four families, with recitation rooms in the first stories. Pairs of professors' houses were connected by one-story colonnades. The three-story Rotunda, apparently inspired by Jefferson's University of Virginia, 1819–26, was seventy-five feet in diameter, encircled by twenty-four paired Ionic columns, with a pedimented portico and a dome.[18] The Rotunda served as a ceremonial meeting place and library. When Nichols advertised for bricklayers, brickmakers, masons, stonecutters and carpenters in May, 1828, he promised that the final specifications would be ready in June.[19] The University opened three years later, in April, 1831, with four professors and ninety-four students. Except for a dining hall, an observatory, a small guard house and the President's House, built by Michael Barry in 1839–41, all of the original buildings at the University were burned in April, 1865.

William Nichols, like many Southern builders in the late Federal period, was experimenting with monumental Roman forms, especially the Ionic order, in the late 1820's and early 1830's. Nichols's design for Christ Church at Tuscaloosa, 1830, was a pedimented temple with a recessed Ionic portico. Christ Church was remodelled in the Gothic style in 1884. Nichols may have provided the design of The Forks-of-Cypress, built in the late 1820's at the forks of the Big and Little Cypress creeks outside Florence, for James Jackson, an Irish-born pioneer, land speculator, planter and surveyor who came to Alabama through Philadelphia and Nashville. In 1814 Jackson purchased large tracts of land in Lauderdale County and moved to Florence. A friend of Andrew Jackson, James Jackson was famous for his stable of race horses and was related by marriage to several prominent Southern families. The Forks, a box-like two-story frame building with a wide semicircular fanlight entrance, was surrounded by a monumental colonnade of twenty-four Ionic columns, the only example of a peripteral temple in Alabama. The Forks burned in 1966. Nichols may also have built or influenced the design of the James Dearing House, 421 Queen City Avenue, Tuscaloosa, c. 1834–35, for a merchant and steamboat captain who came to Alabama in 1819 from North Carolina and served as a member of the building committee for the Tuscaloosa Capitol, and the Alexander Dearing House, 2111 14th Street, Tuscaloosa, c. 1838, for James's brother, a planter. In December, 1833, Nichols moved from Alabama to New Orleans.

University of Alabama, Tuscaloosa, Alabama, 1828–31, as pictured on a sheet music cover of 1839. *University of Alabama Library*

Christ Church, Tuscaloosa, Alabama, c. 1830, a 19th-century view before its Gothic renovation. *University of Alabama Library*

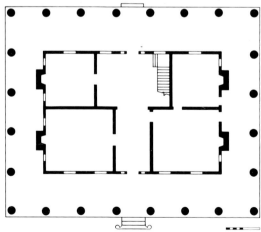

The-Forks-of-Cypress, James Jackson House, Florence, Alabama, vicinity, c. 1830. *Photograph by Frances Benjamin Johnston, Library of Congress*

James Dearing House, 421 Queen City Avenue, Tuscaloosa, Alabama, c. 1834–35, a 19th-century photograph. *University of Alabama Library*

III. *The Greek Revival*

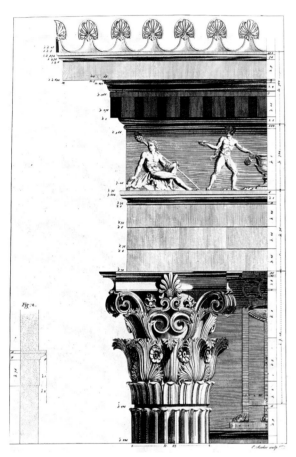

Choragic Monument of Lysicrates, Plate VI of James Stuart and Nicholas Revett's *Antiquities of Athens* (London, 1762), the model specified by William Nichols for Corinthian capitals at Mississippi State Capitol. *Art & Architecture Collection, Miriam & Ira D. Wallach Division of Art, Prints and Photographs, The New York Public Library, Astor, Lenox and Tilden Foundations*

"The holiest and most magnificent ruin the world contains . . . inimitable and uninterrupted perfection extended to its minutest parts—the flutings of the columns, the swelling of the capitals, and all the endless ornaments of the architrave, frieze and cornice!" Thus was the Parthenon described by a newspaper at Tuscaloosa, Alabama, in April, 1831.[1] The Greek Revival was the most widespread and genuinely popular architectural style of 19th-century America and, with its massive, shady porticoes, was well suited to the Southern climate. Though it was an expression of the nation's democratic ideals and of sympathy for the Greeks during their rebellion against the Turks in the 1820's, the movement was not particularly American, and, though great white columns are associated in the popular mind with the Old South, the Greek Revival was not particularly Southern.

The Greek Revival had begun to sweep across the entire Western World, as far east as St. Petersburg and as far west as Philadelphia, in the late 18th century. An English work, James Stuart and Nicholas Revett's *Antiquities of Athens*, whose first three volumes appeared between 1762 and 1794, illustrated the ancient monuments that became icons of 19th-century Greek Revival architecture. Among these were the 4th-century Corinthian Monument of Lysicrates, the 5th-century Ionic Temple on the Ilissus and the 1st-century Tower of the Winds. When Ezra Williams was hired to carve the columns for the interior of the new Capitol at Jackson, Mississippi, in 1837, he was instructed by the architect, the English-born William Nichols, to model his work on the Monument of Lysicrates, the Tower of the Winds and the Erechtheion at Athens "as shown in detail in engravings in a work known as Stewart's 'Antiquities of Athens.'"[2] William Nichols's work in the late 1820's had presaged the full flowering of the Greek Revival in Alabama and Mississippi.

The expansion of the Old Southwest in the 1830's coincided with the spread of Greek Revival architecture throughout America. In this decade the last Creek, Choctaw, Chickasaw and Cherokee indians were removed from central Mississippi and Alabama, millions of acres of fertile lands were opened to eager cotton farmers, and a new wave of immigration from the upper and coastal South flooded into the area. The lawyer Joseph G. Baldwin described these flush times in Alabama and Mississippi: "This country was just settling up, marvellous accounts had gone forth of the fertility of its virgin lands. Emigrants came flooding in from all quarters of the Union. The new country seemed to be a reservoir and every road leading to it a vagrant stream of enterprise and adventure!"[3]

Mobile, located some twenty-five miles up a large bay from the Gulf of Mexico, had been captured by the Americans during the War of 1812. During the 1830's, as the Alabama hinterland began to flourish, Mobile enjoyed spectacular growth. During the decade, Mobile's population increased from 3194 to 12,672, and the city became second only to New Orleans in importance as a cotton port. Much of the old town, which burned in 1827, was being rebuilt with brick, and the site of the old French fort in the center of town was sold to speculators who laid out new lots for building. Melissa Russell, the sister of an Indian agent from Massachusetts, described Mobile in 1835: "It is a *growing* city certainly, for every street is filled with lumber and bricks for building new or altering the old blocks."[4] In January, 1835, there were forty vessels loading cotton in the harbor and most of them were from New York. Mobile was attracting settlers as well as ships from the North. The first American mayor of Mobile came from Connecticut, and other prominent New Englanders included Thaddeus Sanford, a Connecticut-born merchant and newspaper editor, William Ledyard, a cotton broker from New York, Charles Dickey, the agent for Brown Brothers of New York, William Hallett, a New York banker, Moses Waring, a cotton merchant from Connecticut, Archibald Gordon, a land speculator from Connecticut, and, most important of all, Henry Hitchcock, a lawyer and entrepreneur from Burlington, Vermont, who became the first Attorney General of Alabama. In 1850, when the first census was made listing the birthplace of citizens, of 310 carpenters in Mobile, 111 were foreigners, seventy-four came from New England, New York and Pennsylvania, nine came from the Midwest, while only forty-eight came from Alabama and the states of the Mississippi Valley and the Gulf coast and sixty-eight came from elsewhere in the upper and seaboard South.

In the mid-1830's, three gifted young architects who had worked in New York—James Gallier, James Dakin and his brother Charles Dakin—decided to seek professional opportunities in the burgeoning Mississippi Valley.[5] James Gallier (1798–1866) was an Irish-born, professionally trained architect who had worked in London before coming to New York in 1832, where he worked with James Dakin and Minard Lafever. James

Corinthian capital, Senate Chamber, Mississippi State Capitol, Jackson, 1837.

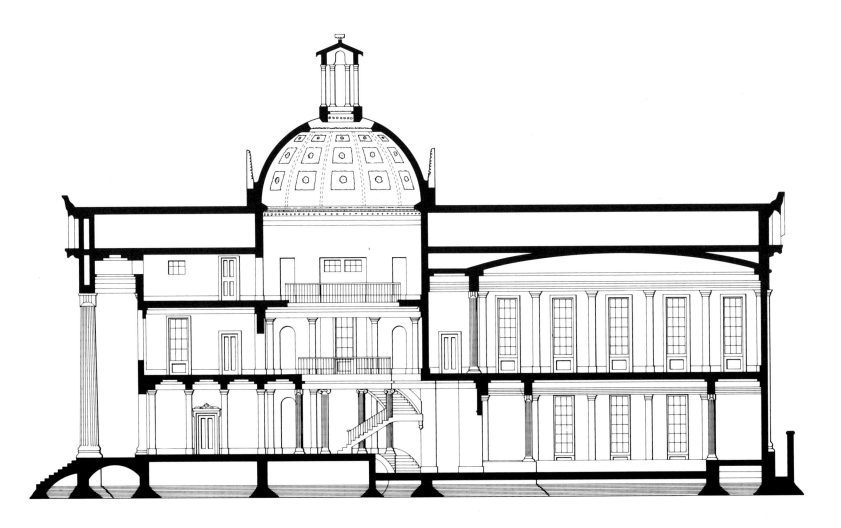

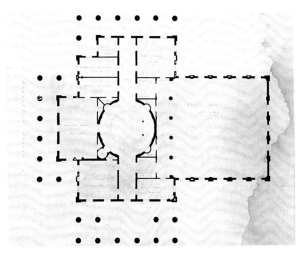

Designs for proposed City Hall, Mobile, Alabama, by James Gallier and Charles Dakin, 1834–35. Sectional view redrawn from a lost original. *Plan from New Orleans Public Library*

Dakin (1806–1852) and his brother Charles (1811–1839) were born in Dutchess County, New York. James Dakin had learned the building trade in the traditional manner by working for his guardian, a carpenter named Herman Stoddard, but James Dakin was a gifted draftsman, described by Gallier in his memoirs as "a young man of genius." James and Charles Dakin had worked in the office of Ithiel Town and Alexander Jackson Davis in New York City.

In October, 1834, Gallier and Charles Dakin boarded a steamer bound for New Orleans. When the ship called at Mobile, they heard that yellow fever was raging in the Louisiana delta and decided to wait out the sick season by remaining in Mobile. During several weeks of delay, the young architects were introduced to the sympathetic Yankee leaders of Mobile, foremost among them Henry Hitchcock, and found a rich and eager clientele and little professional competition. Gallier and Charles Dakin received $300 for drawings for a new City Hall planned for a site on Bienville Square. The Gallier and Dakin drawings illustrate a three-story cruciform structure with a portico, rotunda and dome, combining monumental grandeur with unexpected freedom of functional planning. Their design was not used after all, and a more modest plan provided by a brickmason named Thomas Ellison was finally employed. Gallier and Charles Dakin soon proceeded to New Orleans, where they set up an office on Canal Street, but they had already begun other designs for Mobile.

Henry Hitchcock, a member of the building committee, probably brought Gallier and Charles Dakin the commission for Government Street Presbyterian Church, which was built at 300 Government Street in 1835–37 by Thomas James, a Virginia-born bricklayer, and R. J. Barnes. Like several buildings by Town and Davis in New York, Government Street Church features a recessed Ionic portico flanked by pilasters. Inside, the auditorium's wide, flat ceiling is supported by a wooden truss, an invention of Ithiel Town that was as useful for creating squarish, flat-roofed Greek Revival buildings as for erecting bridges spanning long distances. As a deliberate gesture of religious symbolism, a temple-like reredos rises behind the pulpit like a propylaeum, the entrance to ancient sacred precincts. The Corinthian capitals and anthemia of this reredos are copied from Plates 43 and 44 of Minard Lafever's *Beauties of Modern Architecture*, one of the most popular architectural books of the period. The Greek frets on the balcony, details for the columns supporting the balcony and carved scrolls on the pews were copied from Lafever's Plate 48. Charles Dakin's copy of *The Beauties of Modern Architecture* has survived. The Government Street Presbyterian Church was completed in time for Charles Dakin's marriage, in March, 1837. The steeple was blown down in 1852.

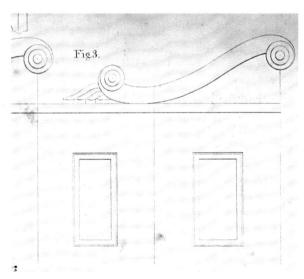

Plate 48 of Minard Lafever's *Beauties of Modern Architecture* (New York, 1835), model for balcony frets and columns at Government Street Presbyterian Church, Mobile, Alabama, 1835–37. *Private Collection*

Government Street Presbyterian Church, 300 Government Street, Mobile, Alabama, 1835–37, a view of c. 1900. *Wilson Collection, Historic Mobile Preservation Society*

Government Street Presbyterian Church, interior view.

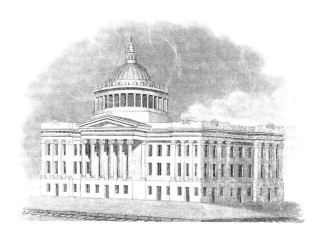

Barton Academy, Mobile, Alabama, 1835–38, seen in vignette on John La Tourette's 1838 map of Mobile and a photograph c. 1930. *Map illustration from Map Division, Library of Congress; photograph from Erik Overbey Collection, University of South Alabama Archives*

Henry Hitchcock was also a member of the school board, a principal contributor to the fund for a new educational hall and a member of its building committee. The edifice, with space for public and semi-public educational activities, was named Barton Academy in honor of Willoughby Barton, author of the legislative bill that established public education at Mobile in 1826. Gallier and Charles Dakin's design for the Academy featured a raised two-story Ionic portico, a dome encircled by Ionic columns and a lantern modelled on the Lantern of Demosthenes, one of the icons of Greek Revival architecture. The Academy, at 504 Government Street, was completed by Thomas James, builder of the Government Street Church, in 1838. The interior of the Academy has been remodelled for city offices.

In November, 1835, James Dakin joined his brother Charles in the South. While James Gallier began a successful independent career in New Orleans, the Dakins formed a new partnership. James remained in New Orleans, but work was so busy in Mobile that Charles opened a permanent office in Mobile in December, 1835. Large hotels were a new building type in America, and ambitious cities were competing to produce the largest and most luxurious hostelry. Henry Hitchcock was an investor in the new Government Street Hotel and owned the land on which it was to be built. The Dakin brothers' design for the Government Street Hotel was virtually identical with undated ones they submitted for a hotel in New Orleans that was never built. These designs, in turn, were based on an 1832 study that James Dakin had made for a hotel in New York. The Hotel was four stories over a raised basement, with a recessed Ionic portico flanked by monumental pilasters. Windows were set between these giant pilasters and treated as a single vertical shaft, a variation on the "Davisean" windows created by A. J. Davis in New York. A dome was encircled by a colonnade of Corinthian columns and surmounted by a tall lantern. The Government Street Hotel was begun by Thomas James in July, 1836. Though it was the second largest hotel anywhere in the nation at the time of its construction, this magnificent building is little known because it was destroyed by fire in 1839.

Henry Hitchcock helped raise capital for the new Planters and Merchants Bank, which was established in January, 1836. The Dakin brothers were asked to provide the design—a boxy, two-story stuccoed building fronted with square pillars, or antae, and surmounted by a shallow dome. Alternate studies by the Dakins employed the Doric and Ionic orders. The Bank was begun in 1837 and completed in 1838. The interior was enriched with marble paving, panelling, marble counters, fretwork, fluted columns and a domed ceiling. The Bank also burned in 1839.

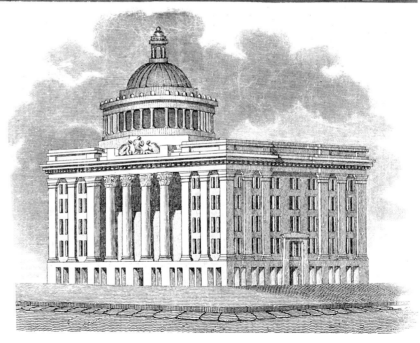

Study for a hotel, by James Dakin, c. 1832, with Government Street Hotel, Mobile, Alabama, 1835–39, from La Tourette map. *Drawing from New Orleans Public Library; map illustration from Map Division, Library of Congress*

Studies for the Planters and Merchants Bank, Mobile, Alabama, by James Dakin, 1836.
New Orleans Public Library

Charles Dakin's surviving account book lists many other projects in Mobile—houses, stores, offices, another hotel, a cotton press, a hospital—but further knowledge of these buildings has been lost. Christ Church, 114 St. Emanuel Street, is not mentioned in the account book but may have been designed by the Dakins. The distinctive recessed portico flanked by pilasters was a design that had been popularized by Town and Davis in New York. In November, 1835, the building committee of Christ Church considered two plans—one Gothic and one Greek Doric—but no action was taken until another Greek Doric design was submitted in May, 1838. As construction was beginning, Charles Dakin left Mobile, so supervision was put in the hands of Cary W. Butt (c. 1797–1844), a Virginia-born architect who had worked with Charles Dakin. The builder, James Barnes (probably the same "R. J. Barnes" who was one of the builders of the Government Street Church), completed Christ Church in 1841. Its steeple collapsed in a 1906 hurricane, which also destroyed the roof and interior ceiling. A smaller building of related design, its designer unidentified, was the now-demolished Unitarian Church on Jackson Street, built in 1836–37.

In 1837 a financial panic, accompanied by a collapse in the price of cotton and bank failures, curtailed Mobile's prosperity. In the fall of 1839 a yellow fever epidemic claimed Henry Hitchcock as one of its victims, and a rash of fires destroyed some 1300 buildings, including the new Government Street Hotel and the Planters and Merchants Bank. Business was so disrupted that Charles Dakin returned to New Orleans in 1838. He died the following year. James Dakin continued to practice architecture in Louisiana and was supervising construction of his masterwork, the Gothic-style Capitol at Baton Rouge, at the time of his death in 1852.

In the 1830's, Natchez, located at the center of the rich and well-established cotton lands along the lower Mississippi River, continued the prosperity that had begun in the late 1790's. As the cultivation of cotton spread to the river parishes of Louisiana, north to the Mississippi delta and into Arkansas and Texas, Natchez remained a vital economic and social center, although the town never grew to spectacular size. In the 1830's, the population was some 2800 people, and the streets were still unpaved except for brick sidewalks and large logs thrown across the intersections. "Buildings are going up in every part of the city," reported the newspaper, "carpenters and joiners, painters, &c. have more work than they can accomplish [and] are realizing fortunes."[6] The Agricultural Bank on Main Street, the earliest Greek Revival building in Mississippi, was built in 1833–34.[7] Despite its faulty proportions and unorthodox use of paired columns, the temple-like Bank made a sensation. The designer of the Bank

Washington Fire Engine Company Station, 7 North Lawrence Street, Mobile, Alabama, c. 1851, a 19th-century view. *Historic Mobile Preservation Society*

Christ Church, 114 St. Emanuel Street, Mobile, 1835–40, seen in an 1840 lithograph and a photograph before 1906 hurricane. *Lithograph from Library of Congress; Photograph from Wilson Collection, Historic Mobile Preservation Society*

Unitarian Church, Mobile, Alabama, 1836–37, a photograph of c. 1900. *Erik Overbey Collection, University of South Alabama Archives*

Agricultural Bank, Main Street, Natchez, Mississippi, 1833–34, a photograph of c. 1890. *Private Collection*

Ravenna, William Harris House, 601 South Union Street, Natchez, Mississippi, 1835–36. *Restored elevation by Melanie Wilson*

is unidentified. One of several possible architects was a mysterious "Mr. Brown" from New York who declared himself eager to prepare "designs, plans, specifications, estimates and working drawings for Churches, Court Houses, Banks, Hotels and other public buildings and city and country dwellings, and superintend their erection."[8] Another possible designer of the Bank was J. C. Deadmore, an experienced "practical builder and architect" who offered to draw plans and elevations "together with linear and perspective drawings of any variety and description, to any given order of architecture."[9]

Another new talent was Peter Gemmell who, born in Scotland in 1805, came to Natchez in 1830 at the age of twenty-five.[10] With his partner Joseph Neibert, Gemmell was the builder of Ravenna, the home of William Harris, a cotton merchant, at 601 South Union Street in 1835–36. Ravenna's two-tiered portico employs superimposed orders—Doric capitals on the first story and Ionic capitals on the second story. A visitor walks into a central hall and, beneath an arch supported by pairs of Doric columns, to a spiral stair. This spiral stair, not typical of the Greek Revival, indicates Ravenna's importance in the transition from the Federal to the Greek Revival styles. After a brief career, Gemmell died at Natchez in 1837.[11]

T. J. Hoyt also came to Natchez in the 1830's, a practical builder and architect ready to make "Plans, Geometrical, Perspective, Elevations, Skeleton or Detail Working Drawings of Buildings . . . in the most approved modern style of architecture [the Greek Revival]."[12] Hoyt designed The Burn, a frame cottage at 307 Oak Street, for John P. Walworth, a planter-merchant who had come to Mississippi from Aurora, New York, by way of Cleveland about 1820. The builders of The Burn, erected in 1836–37, were David Montgomery and Chancey Keyes. The front door case was copied from Plate 28 of Asher Benjamin's *Practical House Carpenter*, published at Boston in 1830.

Levin R. Marshall, a relentlessly aggressive entrepreneur from Virginia, came to Natchez about 1817 and accumulated great wealth, including a hotel, a steamship, a bank and 25,000 acres of land in Mississippi, Louisiana and Arkansas. In 1838 the veteran builder Andrew Brown, who was active in Natchez for some forty years, erected for Marshall the Commercial Bank on Main Street, an elegant Ionic temple of gray marble and stuccoed brick. The Bank is the only antebellum building in Mississippi with a façade of finished stone. Brown was probably not the building's designer, for Thomas Henderson, the bank cashier, had already received the plans and specifications before he advertised for builders in December, 1837. In the early 19th century, a bank officer was expected to provide personal security for his depositors by living on the premises, so the Com-

Ravenna, view of hall leading to stair.

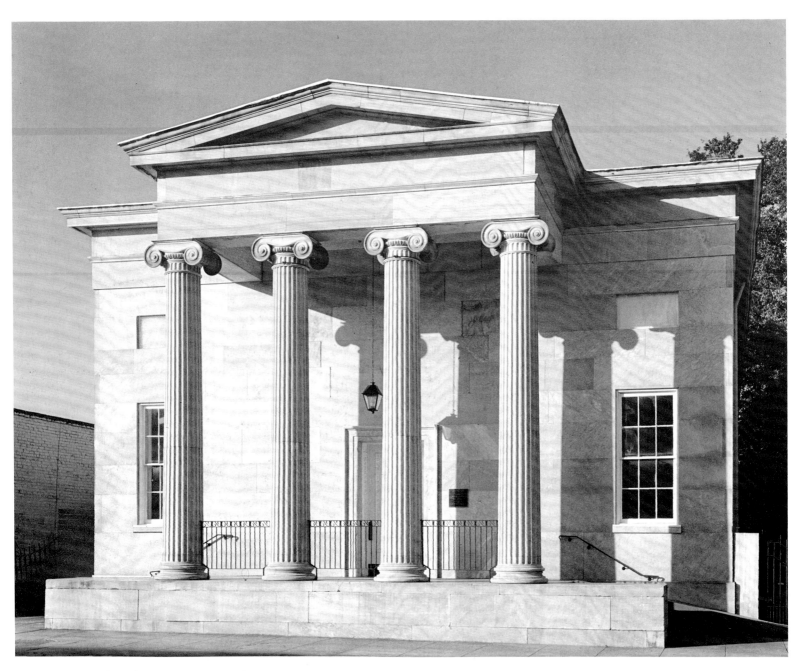

Commercial Bank, Main Street, Natchez, Mississippi, 1838.

mercial Bank building incorporates a residence for the cashier.

In 1832, Marshall had purchased Richmond, a traditional late-18th-century raised cottage a few miles outside the center of Natchez. Perhaps it was the same talented but unidentified designer of the Commercial Bank who added a wing with an Ionic portico at the southern end of this cottage in the late 1830's? In the parlors of this new wing, fluted pilasters flank door and window openings. In the old cottage, which was partially remodelled, two small rooms were joined by a new screen of fluted Doric pillars with folding doors. At an undetermined date, perhaps as early as the 1840's, another two-story addition was made at the north end of the old cottage. Another important remodelling project of the late 1830's was Trinity Church, at 305 South Commerce Street. Built in the Federal style in 1822, Trinity was given a new Doric portico in 1838–40 by the builders Mark Breedon and Pennsylvania-born Charles Reynolds.

Jacob Byers (1800–1852), a carpenter who had come to Mississippi from Hagerstown, Maryland, by the mid-1830's, was the builder and designer of Melrose, a two-story brick mansion with a Doric portico, for a lawyer from Pennsylvania, John T. McMurran, about 1845. Melrose's unusual plan is arranged around an interior central hall, which still retains its original painted floorcloth. The stair is set in a lateral passage, a practice often favored in the large mansions of Natchez. Doorways are framed by engaged Ionic columns. Though Byers, who worked for the builders Neibert and Gemmell, must have had a hand in many projects, no other buildings can be associated with him.

Natchez was many miles up the Mississippi River from the Gulf of Mexico, but the city was so important a port that it was chosen as the site of one of the Marine Hospitals erected by the Federal government for the care of sick sailors. Its design was provided by Robert Mills, who described himself as the first native-born professionally trained architect in America. Mills (1781–1855) had left his home, Charleston, South Carolina, to work with James Hoban, designer of the White House, at Washington. In 1836 President Andrew Jackson appointed Mills as Architect and Engineer for the U.S. Government, and in that capacity Mills prepared model designs for marine hospitals in 1837. The larger of these, adapted for use at Natchez, featured an H-shaped plan, projecting corner pavilions, a cupola, fire-resistant construction and three-tiered galleries on which patients could recuperate. Construction was supervised by Stephen H. Long (1784–1864), a career army officer who also superintended construction of three other hospitals on the Mississippi—at Louisville and Paducah, Kentucky, and Napoleon, Arkansas. The Marine Hospital at Natchez was built in 1849–52 and burned in 1984.

Trinity Church, 305 South Commerce Street, Natchez, Mississippi, 1822, with Doric portico added in 1838–40.

D'Evereux. William St. John Elliot House, Natchez, Mississippi, c. 1835.

This page and opposite: Exterior views of Richmond, Levin Marshall House, Natchez, Mississippi, a late-18th-century cottage enlarged c. 1840 and c. 1850.

This page and opposite: Views of parlors and dining room at Richmond.

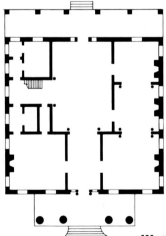

Melrose, John T. McMurran House, Natchez, Mississippi, c. 1845, with its plan.

Melrose, view of parlors.

In December, 1833, William Nichols had moved from Alabama to New Orleans as Assistant State Engineer of Louisiana. During his long career, stretching between his arrival in North Carolina in 1800 and his death in Mississippi in 1853, Nichols demonstrated an eagerness to absorb new trends of architectural style. We have already seen how Nichols had favored monumental Roman forms in general and details of the Roman Ionic order in particular when he worked as a young man in North Carolina and Alabama. His 1827 design for the Alabama State House at Tuscaloosa was a Palladian palace, but it was embellished with several specifically Greek details, including Corinthian capitals that were described (probably by the architect) as looking "as natural as the acanthus plant on the tomb of the Athenian Maiden, from which Callimachus first took his idea of the order."[13] While in New Orleans, Nichols must have admired the "modern" Greek buildings of Gallier and James Dakin and, thus emboldened, pursued Greek design with new enthusiasm when he moved to Mississippi in late 1835.

Though Jackson had been the capital of Mississippi since 1822, the town had remained a mere village until the state government was reorganized ten years later. In 1833, the legislature authorized the construction of new public buildings and Governor Charles Lynch appointed John Lawrence, a builder from Nashville, as State Architect.[14] Construction of a new Capitol began in 1834 under Lawrence's direction, but Lawrence had neither the knowledge nor talent for such an enormous undertaking, and, after more than a year of confusion and delay, he was dismissed in October, 1835. William Nichols applied for the position, boasting to the Governor that he had "more experience in the construction of state Capitols than any other individual in the Union." Nichols received the appointment as Mississippi State Architect in November, 1835. Though the census records state that John Lawrence was living in Clinton, Mississippi, in 1850, his later career is unknown.

Reaching Jackson in early 1836, Nichols redesigned the Capitol at Jackson and supervised its construction, which continued to be plagued by poor workmanship and was further delayed by the Panic of 1837, which crippled the state's finances for several years. In March, 1836, the building commissioners discovered that the mason Edward Moody had been laying the foundations with broken and half-burned bricks and weak mortar, and they ordered the walls torn down and rebuilt. Nichols advertised for craftsmen in the newspapers of Jackson, Vicksburg, Natchez, Huntsville, Nashville, New Orleans, Louisville, Cincinnati, Pittsburgh and New York. Bricks were made by James B. Joplin, William S. Orr and Landy Lindsey. John Robb from North Carolina supplied decorative stonework

Mississippi State Capitol, Jackson, Mississippi, 1836–39, detail from a map of Mississippi by T. C. Story. *University of Mississippi Library*

State Capitol, Jackson, Mississippi, first-story doorway.

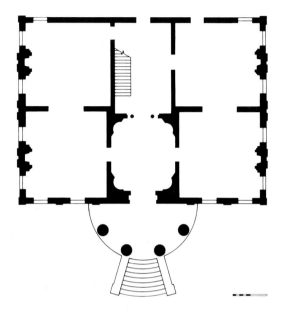

Plan of the Governor's Mansion, Jackson, Mississippi.

Plate 26 of Minard Lafever's *Beauties of Modern Architecture* (New York, 1835), model for doorways at the Governor's Mansion. *Private Collection*

for the exterior, including pilasters, capitals, sills and lintels. Ezra Williams, the carver from New Orleans, produced the intricate capitals for the interior. Alexander Baird, another stonemason, came from Virginia. The plasterers Caleb A. Parker and Robert Moors and the tinsmith Martin H. Devereux also came from New Orleans.[15] Though the legislature first met at the Capitol in January, 1839, scaffolding shrouded the building and rubbish cluttered the Capitol square until the following December. When the building, by then abandoned by the state legislature, was renovated in 1916–17, the old House and Senate chambers were destroyed to make space for state offices. An extensive renovation in 1959–61 recreated the general appearance of these rooms, but only six Corinthian capitals in the Senate chamber, the speaker's rostrum in the House, portions of the Rotunda and the doorways along the first-floor corridors are intact from the original building. The Mississippi Capitol of 1836–39 is open to the public.

While the Capitol was under construction, Nichols began work on a Governor's Mansion at 316 East Capitol Street in Jackson. The architect reported to the legislature that his design—a two-story brick structure that was unadorned except for pilasters, stone trim and a monumental semicircular Corinthian portico—was intended to "avoid a profusion of ornament and to adhere to a plain republican simplicity."[16] The foundations were being dug in September and October, 1839. Stephen D. Howell and Messrs. Walker and McLachlan completed the masonry work in the fall of 1840. The interior carpentry was by Reuben Clark, with ornamental carving and plasterwork by William Gibbons and Ezra Williams, who had worked at the Capitol. Like other builders, William Nichols turned to books as important sources for "correct" designs. The capitals for the portico of the Governor's Mansion were copied from Plate 43 of Minard Lafever's *Beauties of Modern Architecture*. Interior doorways were copied from Lafever's Plate 26, and mantels were copied from Plate 46. The Mansion was first occupied by Governor Tilghman Tucker in 1842. In the early 1900's the exterior walls were refaced with the pale yellow brick that was then so popular. In 1975 the interior was extensively renovated (including the conjectural recreation of the principal staircase, in place of one added in 1909, and removal of an original service stair, to enlarge the dining room) and a two-story rear wing was erected in place of the original one-story residential wing. The Governor's Mansion is open to the public.

Many of the same craftsmen who worked at the Capitol and Mansion also worked at the new State Penitentiary. Nichols had presented his plans for a Gothic-style prison to the authorities in June, 1836. Landy Lindsey, who was already selling bricks to the state for public buildings, agreed to

Governor's Mansion, 316 East Capitol Street, Jackson, Mississippi, 1839–42.

Governor's Mansion, view of entrance hall.

Governor's Mansion, view of parlor doorway.

Lyceum, University of Mississippi, Oxford, Mississippi, 1846–48, a 19th-century view.
University of Mississippi Library

lay the foundations for the Penitentiary after Thomas Harris, from Cincinnati, abandoned his contract. In addition to Lindsey, the principal contractors were Walter St. Clair, brickmaker, A. B. Reading, ironmonger, and Reuben Clark, carpenter. In February, 1840, Nichols reported that the keeper's house, kitchen, laundry, offices, infirmary and 150 cells in the east wing had been completed. The first prisoners arrived in April and were put to work on construction. Nichols's Penitentiary was demolished in 1901.

In late 1838, John Potter, the indefatigable manager of theaters in Nashville, Louisville and Natchez, began raising money to build a new theater in Jackson. It was said that, because a nervous disorder produced glistening tears most of the time in one eye, his emotional appeals to investors were particularly effective. Plans, provided by the obscure F. A. Stafford, were displayed to the public in January, 1839, and the theater was completed at the end of the year.[17] There are no illustrations of this building, but the newspaper described it as "built in the Grecian order of Architecture, having six antaes in front, supporting an entablature and cornice, taken from the Choragic Monument of Thasyllus at Athens."[18]

After his work on the public buildings at Jackson had been completed, Nichols was employed to provide designs for buildings at the University of Mississippi at Oxford and supervise their construction.[19] The architect conferred with the University trustees at their first meeting in January, 1845. The Lyceum, a three-story brick building with a pedimented Ionic portico, was built in 1846–48. It contained lecture halls, a laboratory, a library and museum. Other early buildings at the University included two three-story dormitories (1848 and 1857), two professors' houses (1848) and a steward's hall. The University opened in November, 1848, with five teachers, including the President, and eighty students.

In the late 1850's, the University of Mississippi was reinvigorated by a new chancellor, Frederick A. P. Barnard.[20] Born in Massachusetts and educated at Yale, Barnard taught at the University of Alabama in 1838–54 before coming to Oxford as Professor of Mathematics, Astronomy and Civil Engineering in 1854. He had supervised the design and construction of a small observatory at the University of Alabama in 1834–44 and undertook the building of a much larger observatory at the University of Mississippi in 1859.[21] This was a sprawling two-story structure with a functional plan containing classrooms, laboratories, a residence for the professor of physics and astronomy and a gigantic telescope. This instrument would have been the largest reflecting telescope in America at the time, but it was never delivered by its manufacturer in Massachusetts because of the coming of the Civil War. Frederick A. P. Barnard returned

Observatory, University of Mississippi, Oxford, Mississippi, 1859, a 19th-century view. *University of Mississippi Library*

to the North in 1861, after having spent twenty-three years in Alabama and Mississippi, and served as President of Columbia University between 1864 and 1889.

In 1849–50 William Nichols designed and built a now-demolished courthouse at Yazoo City, sixty feet square with a Doric portico, flanked by pilasters enriched with Tower-of-the-Winds capitals, surmounted by a Corinthian lantern. In November, 1850, at the age of seventy-three, Nichols was still offering to "furnish designs for residences in every style of Architecture, accompanied by plans, details, specimens, and directions, with a careful and accurate estimate of the cost."[22] Nichols died at Lexington, Mississippi, in 1853, where he is believed to have built the Lexington Female College, a temple-form structure with a Temple-of-the-Winds portico, and the county courthouse, both demolished.

Northern Alabama was also enjoying growth and prosperity in the 1830's. George Steele (1798–1855), who had come to Huntsville as a youth from Bedford County, Virginia, was established as the leading builder of that area by 1830.[23] He also operated a brick kiln and a cotton factory. In October, 1834, Steele offered four or five house carpenters "good wages and constant employment until the 1st of April next."[24] Steele probably designed and built the portico added in the 1830's to Leroy Pope's house, 407 Echols Street, an unadorned two-story, hip-roofed brick building that had been erected in 1814. Steele's Tuscan portico features an unconventional truncated pediment, enriched with an elliptical fanlight and radiating quarter-sunbursts and surmounted by a balustraded deck, from which Pope could have surveyed the growing city of Huntsville in the valley below his mansion.

George Steele may have also been the designer of the Alabama State Bank branch at nearby Decatur, built in 1834–36. Despite its ambitious monumentality, reflecting the Greek Revival, the Bank displays semicircular fanlights, which were so popular during the Federal era, a disconcertingly unorthodox Roman portico with five columns, which was virtually unknown in ancient Classical architecture, and square blocks in place of conventional Doric capitals. Details for the eaves cornice were copied from the sixth edition of Asher Benjamin's *American Builder's Companion*, an old-fashioned pattern book first issued in 1806.

In the spring of 1835, Steele made a long trip to Charlottesville, Washington and Baltimore and had his first chance to see sophisticated buildings by professional architects. In March, 1835, Steele wrote to his father-in-law, Dr. Thomas Fearn, from Washington: "To describe to you what I felt when I first arrived, when the Capitol and the President's Manse, with all their sublimity, broke upon me, would be impossible. . . . I have visited

Leroy Pope House, 407 Echols Street, Huntsville, Alabama, 1814, with portico added c. 1834.

Alabama State Bank, Bank Street, Decatur, Alabama, 1834–36. *Photograph by Frances Benjamin Johnston, Library of Congress*

them several times. . . . On entering these glorious monuments of our national pride . . . I was ready to fall down, and worship, the genius that composed them!"[25] The career of George Steele may be the exception that proves the rule that the greatest Southern architecture was produced by Yankee builders, Yankee books or Yankee influence. His was born in the South, but his taste was enriched and transformed by the sights of his trip to the East.

By September, 1835, Steele had completed plans and specifications for the Alabama State Bank branch at Huntsville.[26] Its splendid "portico of polished stone" demonstrated his new understanding of architectural rectitude. Steele was also the Bank's builder.[27] It was completed, on a lot facing the courthouse square, in 1840. By September, 1836, Steele had also submitted plans for a new Courthouse at Huntsville, described by the building committee as "112 feet in length by 56 feet in width, two stories above the foundation . . . a Doric portico of 6 columns at each end and pilasters at the sides."[28] Steele's design combined a Greek Doric temple and a Roman dome. This architectural *non sequitur* was common among 19th-century designers, both professional and self-taught. The builders, William Wilson and James Mitchell, completed the Courthouse in 1840. It was demolished in 1913–14. In March, 1838, Steele devised a three-story brick hotel, also facing the courthouse square.[29]

Two years later, in 1840, George Steele built a new house for himself at Oak Place on the Maysville Road at the eastern outskirts of Huntsville. This plain, squarish building was originally painted the color of sandstone, with dark burgundy sash. Entering beneath a one-story Doric portico, a visitor discovers a novel split-level plan that isolates private chambers from rooms for entertaining. In 1844 Steele added a similar Doric portico to the house of his father-in-law, Dr. Thomas Fearn, at 517 Franklin Street. Fearn was another of those surprisingly cosmopolitan personalities who ornamented the frontier South. Born in Virginia, Fearn had studied medicine in Philadelphia, London and Paris before moving to isolated northern Alabama.[30] When Steele died in 1855, he owned two slave carpenters, five slave bricklayers, a slave stonecutter and three slave plasterers.

Hiram Harrison Higgins (1802–1874) was a builder who divided his time between Athens, Alabama, where he was listed in the 1850 census as a brickmason, and Talladega, where he was again listed in 1850 as an architect. Born in Sterling, Kentucky, the son of a builder from Virginia, Higgins came to northern Alabama about 1820, at the age of eighteen, with his father and stepmother. Higgins built the Limestone County Courthouse at Athens, a two-story brick structure with a hipped roof and a central tower, in 1833–35 and used a similar design for the Lawrence

Alabama State Bank, Courthouse Square, Huntsville, Alabama, 1835–40.

Madison County Courthouse, Huntsville, Alabama, 1836–40, a photograph made before the demolition of 1913–14. *Library of Congress*

County Courthouse at Moulton in 1859–60. The Limestone Courthouse burned in 1864, the Lawrence Courthouse was demolished in 1935. In 1843–44 Higgins built the main hall at Athens Female College, an institution that had been founded by the Methodists in 1842. The mason was James M. Brundridge from Tennessee and the carpenter was Ira E. Hobbs from Virginia. Higgins's design featured a recessed two-story Ionic portico with a pediment and square bell tower. The pediment and tower were removed when a third story was added to the building in 1892.

In the mid-1840's Hiram Higgins remodelled John Mason's house at 211 South Beatty Street in Athens. The house had been erected in 1826 for Mason's father-in-law, Robert Beatty. Higgins added two details often favored in his work: an Ionic *in antis* portico and three-part windows. After raising a company of soldiers from the neighborhood to fight in the Mexican War in 1847–48, Higgins probably designed the East Alabama Female Institute at 205 East South Street in Talladega, 1850–51, featuring his characteristic Ionic portico flanked by three-part windows. In June, 1859, Higgins described himself as an "architect and superintendent of buildings" who was able to provide "original or copied designs of all kinds of buildings . . . Court-houses, Jails, Fair-grounds, Academy and College Edifices, Private Residences, both plain and ornamental, in all the styles now in use, such as Grecian, Italian, Gothic, Tudor, Elizabethan, Oriental and Castilated."[31]

By the mid-1840's, Montgomery, a flourishing little city of 3800 people, located at the northern edge of Alabama's black belt, a crescent of fertile land stretching across the state, had emerged as a principal trading center for central Alabama. Founded in 1817 on the east bank of the Alabama River, at the head of steamboat navigation, the village had been called New Philadelphia—and also, derisively, "Yankee Town"—because so many Northerners had come there. By 1821, there were forty-nine frame buildings and thirty-eight log buildings and some five hundred people, including "several" carpenters and two bricklayers. In 1845, reflecting the new political and economic importance of the black belt counties, the business leaders of Montgomery offered to pay the cost of erecting a new state house if the legislature would agree to move the capital from Tuscaloosa to Montgomery. After a protracted debate, the legislature finally accepted this proposition and solicited designs.

In April, 1846, the authorities approved plans for a new Capitol that had been submitted by Stephen Decatur Button of Philadelphia. Button (1813–1897) was born at Preston, Connecticut, the son of a farmer.[32] After five years of apprenticeship to a local carpenter, he moved to New York City about 1834. There he worked briefly for the Scottish-born

Athens Female College, Athens, Alabama, 1834–44, a 19th-century woodcut. *Athens College*

John Mason House, 211 South Beatty Street, Athens, Alabama, 1826, with portico added c. 1845. *Photograph by Frances Benjamin Johnston, Library of Congress*

East Alabama Female Institute, 205 East South Street, Talladega, Alabama, 1850–51.
Photograph by Frances Benjamin Johnston, Library of Congress

Alabama State Capitol, Montgomery, Alabama, presentation drawing by Stephen D. Button, 1846. *Alabama Department of Archives and History, Montgomery, Alabama*

architect George Purves. For nine years, from 1835 to 1845, Button worked on the other side of the Hudson River at Hoboken, New Jersey, and at Philadelphia. In 1845 he went to Florida and Georgia, where he designed a church and a house at Columbus, on the Chattahoochee River.[33] Then, in 1846, he won the competition for the design of the Alabama Capitol and moved to Montgomery to supervise its construction. Joseph E. King wrote in June, 1848: "I met the architect, a Mr. Button, from the East. He is a short, strange little fellow. . . . His bottom lip looks like the Hapsburgs, drooping as it does."[34]

Button's presentation drawing of the Capitol, one of those precious architectural artifacts that are so rare in the frontier South, illustrates a stuccoed brick building, two stories over a raised basement, with a pedimented portico flanked by pilasters and surmounted by a dome. The drawing is signed "Stephen D. Button, Arch't, Phila." indicating that the architect considered Philadelphia his home. In the first half of the 19th century, it was not unusual for Northern workmen to come South to find lucrative employment in the mild winter months and return to their families in the North during the torrid summer.

The Capitol's cornerstone was laid in July, 1846, by the builders R.N.R. Bardwell, a thirty-eight-year-old carpenter from Massachusetts, and Bird F. Johnson, a forty-seven-year-old bricklayer from Georgia. In the absence of stone (We have already noted that the only two examples of stone façades in antebellum Mississippi and Alabama were banks at Natchez and Huntsville), skilled stucco artists were employed who could score, pencil, tint and vein stucco to simulate the texture and colors of real stone. The Alabama Capitol's lower walls imitated granite, the upper walls imitated American marble. The exterior stuccoing was supervised by George Gill of New York, a master plasterer who had stuccoed the Hudson River villa of A. J. Downing, the famous horticulturist and architectural writer, who recommended Gill to Charles Crommelin, a New York-born and New York-educated lawyer and art patron who was a member of the Capitol's building committee.[35] In December, 1847, after thirteen wagons carried the state's records from Tuscaloosa to Montgomery, the legislature met for the first time in the new Capitol.

An elaborate newspaper description of the Capitol may have been prepared by the architect: "The main building is 160 feet front by 70 feet deep. The entablature over the Portico is supported by six columns of the Grecian composite style of architecture. The design is taken from Lafever's *Beauties of Modern Architecture*. Directly back of the Portico rises the Dome, 40 feet diameter at the base, rising 20 feet above the apex of the Portico, roof surmounted with a lantern, in imitation of the one at Athens

Plate 11 of Minard Lafever's *Beauties of Modern Architecture* (New York, 1835), model for portico of Alabama State Capitol. *Private Collection*

called the Lantern of Demosthenes. At each end of the main building is a small Portico covering the main entrances to the basement story. These porticoes are supported by 4 columns each of the Grecian Doric order. The example is taken from the Temple of Minerva at Athens, called the Parthenon.

"The floor over the rotunda is supported by 4 Ionic columns, also 2 in the Supreme Court room—the example is taken from the Temple on the Illisseus near Athens. From the hall the grand staircase commences and is continued to the third floor, around a 13-foot hole or cylinder. From the entrance you pass to the rotunda, in the walls of which are 4 openings, supported by two columns each, the example is from the Tower of the Winds at Athens. The Representatives Hall is semicircular, the gallery is supported by 10 Grecian Corinthian columns. The ceiling of this room is domical, panelled with enriched mouldings and a splendid centre flower 10 feet in diameter."[36] The writer's enthusiastic and pedantic references to Greek archaeological sites are typical of the Greek Revival, as are his citation of the most convenient source for these correct details, pattern books like those of New York's Minard Lafever.

In 1847 the old wooden courthouse at Linden, a town of some 150 people, a log jail and two stores, located on the coach road between Mobile and Huntsville, was destroyed by fire. In the following year the authorities hired Erastus Bardwell, a carpenter from Massachusetts, to build a new Courthouse. They may have asked Bardwell to copy the *distyle in antis* buildings of Mobile or printed illustrations of them. An almost identical design was employed by A. J. Davis of New York for the courthouse at Powhatan, Virginia, in the same year, a striking parallel but one without a documented link to the Linden Courthouse of 1848–49. Also undocumented is the connection, if any, between R.N.R. Bardwell of Massachusetts, builder of the 1846–47 Capitol at Montgomery, and Erastus Bardwell of Massachusetts, builder of the Linden Courthouse. There is hope that the Linden Courthouse, long abandoned and decayed, may yet be restored.

In December, 1849, only two years after its construction, the new Capitol at Montgomery burned. In March, 1850, while laborers were clearing away the ruined walls, the authorities began to consider how to rebuild.[37] A design and estimate for a new building were submitted by Daniel Pratt, a builder from New England who had become a pioneering industrialist in Alabama.[38] New Hampshire-born Pratt (1799–1873) had worked as a house carpenter at Savannah and Milledgeville, Georgia, in the late 1820's before moving to Alabama in the mid-1830's, where he manufactured carriages and tinware and operated saw, grist, cotton and

Marengo County Courthouse, Cahaba Avenue, Linden, Alabama, c. 1848. *Library of Congress*

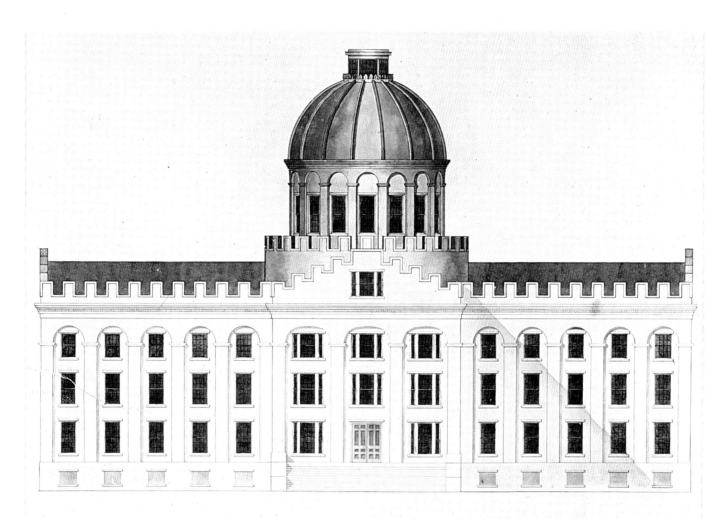

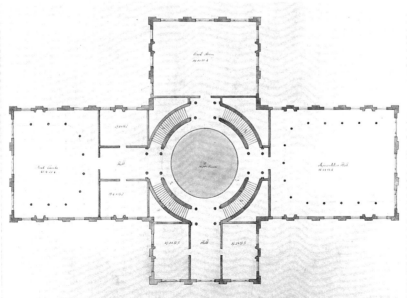

Design for Alabama State Capitol, Montgomery, attributed to Daniel Pratt, 1850.
Alabama Department of Archives and History, Montgomery, Alabama

Alabama State Capitol, Montgomery, Alabama, 1850–51, a view before enlargements of 1906–7. *Alabama Department of Archives and History, Montgomery, Alabama*

Exchange Hotel, Montgomery, Alabama, 1847–49, a 19th-century view. *Library of Congress*

woolen mills and a foundry. Pratt lived at Prattville, the factory town that he built fourteen miles northwest of Montgomery, in a house of his own design that included a separate "gallery of paintings."[39] Pratt had been chairman of one of the committees appointed to inspect Button's new Capitol in November, 1847, and now, two years later, was a commissioner for its rebuilding. The bizarre design attributed to Pratt combined a Classical dome, symbol of American government, Gothic battlements, a traditional symbol of intellectual and spiritual authority, and pilasters joined by shallow relieving arches, a functional and ornamental device popular during the early 19th century.

The commissioners, probably more concerned with cutting costs than with the oddly incongruous combination of Classical and Gothic details in Pratt's design, finally decided to follow the general plan of the old Capitol with modifications suggested by Barachias Holt, a master mechanic from Exeter, Maine, who later became the proprietor of a sash, door and blind factory.[40] The carpentry work was supervised by James D. Randolph from Tennessee, and the brickwork was supervised by John P. Figh of Virginia. Figh (1800–1865) had made the bricks and supervised the laying of the walls at William Nichols's University of Alabama at Tuscaloosa in 1831–32. Figh was also the builder of the Montgomery Courthouse of 1835, the First Presbyterian Church at Montgomery in 1847, the Montgomery Courthouse of 1854 and the Central Bank at Montgomery in 1856.[41] By June, 1850, some one hundred workmen were employed rebuilding the Capitol, and the walls were already four to eight feet high above ground. In April, 1851, the completed structure was stuccoed and scored to simulate blocks of marble. The new Capitol, with an immense town clock replacing the conventional pediment over its portico, was occupied in September, 1851. Wings were added to the east in 1885, to the south in 1906–7 and to the north in 1911–12. The Capitol is now being restored by the State of Alabama.

Stephen Button almost certainly designed Montgomery's Exchange Hotel of 1847–49, a four-story stuccoed brick building with recessed Ionic and Doric porticoes. The major investors in the Hotel were Charles T. Pollard and Charles Crommelin, both of whom were also members of the committee for building the 1846–47 Capitol. The Hotel's builders were B. F. Robinson and R.N.R. Bardwell, contractors for the 1846–47 Capitol. The Exchange Hotel was demolished in 1905. Button was also the probable designer of the William Knox House, 411 South Perry Street, Montgomery, built about 1848 for an Irish-born merchant and banker who had also been a member of the committee for building the 1846–47 Capitol. Decorative details of the interior were copied from Plate 26 of Lafever's

William Knox House, 411 South Perry Street, Montgomery, Alabama, c. 1848. *Alabama Department of Archives and History, Montgomery, Alabama*

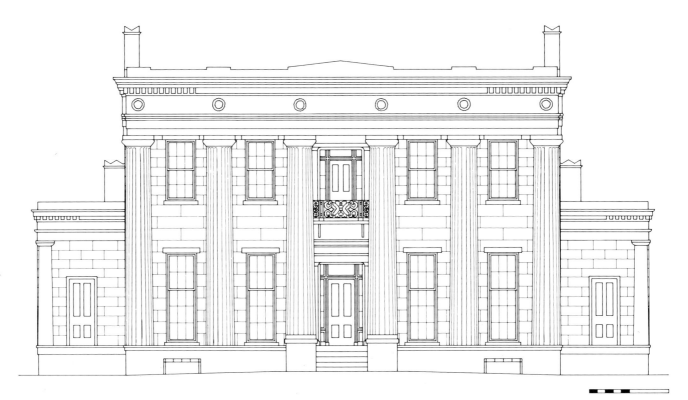

Charles Pollard House, Montgomery, Alabama, 1851–53, with a parlor view. *Photograph from Library of Congress*

Beauties of Modern Architecture. This interior, recorded in an early photograph, was largely destroyed by fire in 1982.

Though Button returned to the North in 1848 to become the partner of his brother-in-law Joseph Hoxie, his reputation had been well established in central Alabama. Like the Dakins in Mobile, he had found a rich and eager clientele and little professional competition. No other documented works by Button appear until Montgomery's Central Bank and Auburn's East Alabama Male College, both 1856, but he probably continued to provide designs by mail, a practice that was common in 19th-century America. Several porticoed mansions of the 1850's in Montgomery and its environs were designed by Button or influenced by his work. The Charles Pollard House on Jefferson Avenue was built in 1851–53 for a banker and railroad investor who had come to Alabama from Virginia and served as a member of the Capitol building committee. Pollard's builder was the same B. F. Randolph who had worked at the 1846–47 Capitol and the Exchange Hotel. Pollard House had interior doorways copied from Lafever's *Beauties of Modern Architecture*. Pollard House was demolished in 1938. The porticoed mansion of John Murphy on Bibb Street, c. 1851, is now used as offices for the city waterworks, and the Thomas Cowles House, built on a site overlooking the Alabama River about 1855, burned in 1908. An early photograph of the Cowles House illustrates the stylish finish given to stuccoed brick buildings in the mid-19th century, their walls scored, penciled, tinted as blocks or veined to suggest the composition of stone.

Button's work may have influenced the design of other porticoed mansions in central Alabama. Dr. Barton Stone's house was built in 1856 on the old road between Montgomery and Selma for a planter from Georgia. Like several of the mansions in Montgomery, the two-story central block of Dr. Stone's house is flanked by recessed one-story wings. Sturdivant Hall, 713 Mabry Street in Selma, was built about 1854–56 for Edward Watts, a Georgia-born planter. The portico is distinguished by Tower-of-the-Winds capitals, but the interior has been substantially changed. Sturdivant Hall is open to the public. The William Cochran House at Tuscaloosa was demolished in 1964 and is undocumented, but the Corinthian portico seen in old photographs clearly dates from the 1850's. William Cochran was a New York-born lawyer.

Benjamin F. Parsons, a builder from Massachusetts, was active in Greene (now Hale), Marengo and Perry counties of Alabama in the 1850's. Born about 1811, Parsons had reached Alabama by 1848. His contract to build a house for Philip Henry Pitts of Uniontown, dated December, 1851, is preserved in the Southern Historical Collection at the University of North

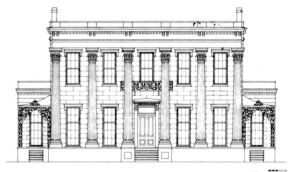

Top: Thomas Cowles House, Montgomery, Alabama, c. 1855. *Alabama Department of Archives and History, Montgomery, Alabama.* Bottom: Dr. Barton Stone House, Montgomery, Alabama, vicinity, 1856.

Sturdivant Hall, Edward Watts House, 713 Mabry Street, Selma, Alabama, c. 1854–56.
Photograph by Frances Benjamin Johnston, Library of Congress

William Cochran House, Tuscaloosa, Alabama, c. 1855. *Photograph by Frances Benjamin Johnston, Library of Congress*

Perry County Courthouse, Marion, Alabama, 1855–56. *University of Alabama Library*

Magnolia Hall, David B. McCrary House, 805 Otts Street, Greensboro, Alabama, c. 1855. *Photograph by Frances Benjamin Johnston, Library of Congress*

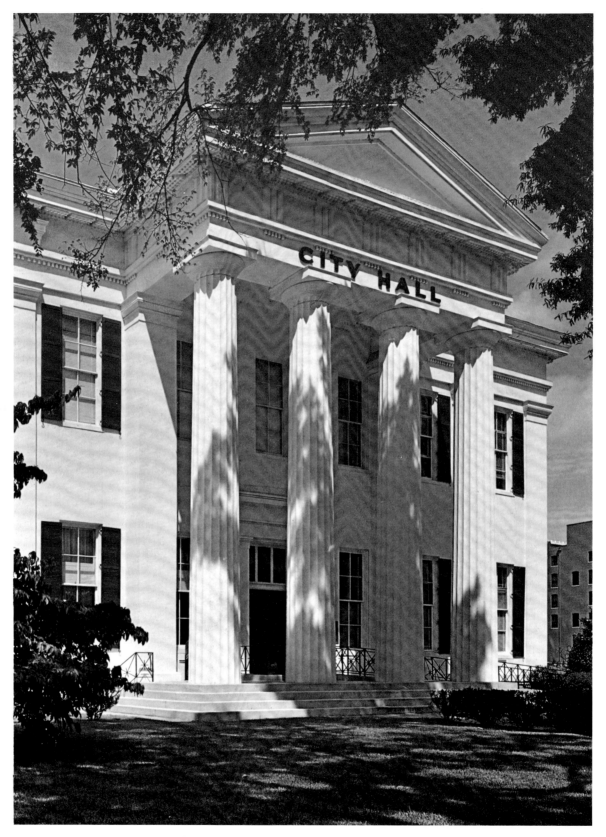

City Hall, 203 South President Street, Jackson, Mississippi, 1846, with portico added 1854.

Carolina. Pitts's Folly, built in 1852–53, features a massive, L-shaped portico running along the full length of the front and left side. Parsons was also the builder of Magnolia Hall, at 805 Otts Street in Greensboro, for David B. McCrary, c. 1855, and the designer of the Perry County Courthouse on the square at Marion, built in 1855–56. In November, 1854, Parsons wrote to the New York architect Richard Upjohn, reporting that he had prepared a plan and specifications for this courthouse, "a two-story, brick building in the Ionic order with circular stairs & porticoes," and asking advice about brick arches.[42] How did the provincial Parsons know the renowned Upjohn? Perhaps Parsons had worked in New York City in the 1840's on his way to Alabama? Parsons supervised construction of the Gothic-style hall of Southern University at Greensboro in 1857–59. Like many other Northern builders, Parsons disappears from the records in 1860, probably because he returned to the North on the eve of the Civil War.

In 1848 the State of Mississippi began construction of a Lunatic Asylum on a site two miles north of Jackson. The architect and builder was William Gibbons, a twenty-eight-year-old, native-born Mississippian who had helped complete the brickwork at William Nichols's Capitol in 1838, plastered the Governor's Mansion in 1841–42, built the City Hall at 203 South President Street at Jackson in 1846–47 and listed himself as an "architect" in the 1850 census. After two years of slow progress, plagued by rainy weather and limited supplies of brick and stone, Gibbons was discharged.

Lunatic Asylum, Jackson, Mississippi, 1848–1854, a 19th-century woodcut. *Private Collection*

His successor was Joseph Willis, a twenty-seven-year-old brickmason from Camden, New Jersey, who arrived in July, 1850. A new mental hospital, a model institution built according to the reformist principles of Dr. Thomas Kirkbride of Philadelphia, had just been completed at Trenton, New Jersey. Perhaps Willis, whose reports demonstrate a detailed familiarity with the New Jersey Asylum, had worked on that building and been recommended by the authorities at Trenton to the building committee in Mississippi? Because the work on the Mississippi asylum had been suspended for several months, Willis found the open cellar of the incomplete building filled with rain water and ordered his workmen to tear down the rotten foundations. Although obliged to follow Gibbons's general plan, Willis altered the internal arrangement of the wings and, he later reported, "somewhat changed the architecture of the building externally." Further delayed by yellow fever among the workmen, the Mississippi Lunatic Asylum was finally completed in 1854. A four-story central building, with a Doric portico and a dome, was flanked by long three-story wings, terminating in four-story pavilions enriched with pilasters and a dentil cornice. This palatial façade was more than three hundred feet long. Cast-iron gutters for the Asylum were supplied by Jabez Reynolds of Cincinnati.[43] The Asylum was abandoned by the State of Mississippi in 1935.

In 1854 Willis enlarged, or substantially rebuilt, Jackson's City Hall, which had been erected eight years earlier at 203 South President Street by William Gibbons. The Masons had petitioned to add a third story as their meeting hall, and the aldermen decided to lengthen the building as well. The Doric portico was probably added by Willis. In early 1854 Willis put a new roof on the Governor's Mansion and erected an iron fence around the property. In 1854 Willis and Allen Patrick, a forty-year-old carpenter from Tennessee, were paid $400 for the design of a Courthouse at Canton. Like the Lunatic Asylum, this design featured Doric porticoes, engaged columns, pilasters, an elaborate entablature and a dome. Upon completion of the Courthouse in 1858, Willis moved to Memphis, Tennessee. His later work included two mental hospitals at Indianapolis, another at Little Rock, and an Episcopal church and a courthouse at Bolivar, Tennessee.[44] Willis was one of the most intriguing talents of early architecture in the Old Southwest, and we are eager to learn more about this gifted, self-confident but little-known personality.

As we have already noted, Irish merchants and builders were important in antebellum Mississippi. The Weldon brothers, a family of Irish builders, came to Jefferson County, Mississippi, by way of Canada about 1835. The brothers were George, born in Ireland about 1805, Thomas, born in Ireland in 1816, and William, born in Canada about 1822. They were master mechanics in Natchez and owners of a sawmill at nearby Rodney. Because they employed a large work force, the Weldons constructed many public buildings, including the jail at Port Gibson, c. 1845, a courthouse at Plaquemine, Louisiana, 1848, the Institute Hall at Natchez, 1851–53, and the Hinds County Courthouse at Raymond, 1857–59. Patrick Murphy, an Irish carpenter and bridge builder who emigrated through New Orleans in 1852 and then worked for the Weldons at Port Gibson and Rodney in the 1850's, noted in his diary that the Weldon brothers received the contract for the Raymond Courthouse only after Joseph Willis, who was completing the Courthouse at Canton and preparing to move to Tennessee, declined the work.[45]

The Weldons' greatest building is the Courthouse at Vicksburg, a bustling railroad city with a population of some 4500 people in 1860. The Courthouse was built in 1858–60 to replace an old structure that had burned in 1857. The new building, designed with the assistance of John Jackson, a black draftsman whom the Weldons employed, featured four two-story Ionic porticoes, balconies, an octagonal clock tower, and iron

Madison County Courthouse, Canton, Mississippi, 1854–58.

Hinds County Courthouse, Raymond, Mississippi, 1857–59.

Warren County Courthouse, Vicksburg, Mississippi, 1858–60, a 19th-century view.
Old Courthouse Museum, Vicksburg

Dr. Grover House, Weaver, Alabama, vicinity, un-documented, c. 1845, an untutored country carpenter's idea of the Greek Revival. *Library of Congress*

shutters, iron window frames, iron doors, iron stairs and iron portico capitals. The building is flanked by four castellated cistern houses. When the Courthouse was remodelled in the 1890's, the exterior was restuccoed to simulate blocks of vermiculated stone. The Courthouse now serves as a museum and archives.[46]

The Weldons were reported to have trained more than one hundred black carpenters and brickmasons. The contribution of black artisans to the architecture of the Old South, especially the anonymous figures who unquestionably provided most of the labor, may never be fully appreciated. In the absence of documentation, this contribution should be neither exaggerated nor slighted. In 1833 a Natchez newspaper reported the attempted suicide of a slave carpenter named Peck, who had been found almost dead, "resting upon his knees and elbows, with his throat open from ear to ear." Asked to explain why he had wounded himself, Peck replied that he "could not stand being whipped to death!"[47]

Across 19th-century Mississippi and Alabama, a land of forests, farms, villages and only a handful of cities, most buildings were simply thrown up quickly for utility and without any pretension of style. When grandeur was attempted, the effort was usually left in the hands of a country carpenter who learned his skills from apprenticeship and experience instead of academic training. A few Greek columns might simply be added to a vernacular building. But, with a bit of courage, the country carpenter could create a more convincing temple-like house by placing a columned portico on the short side of a building and running a pediment from its low-pitched gable roof. Southern builders, having realized that it was necessary to shade southern and western walls from the sun, had already begun to experiment with porches, verandahs and more monumental colonnades in the 1820's. Mississippi and southern Alabama endure the longest and hottest summers in the South, and they were both settled principally by second-generation Southerners from the upper and coastal South where builders had already learned how to adapt to the warm climate. Thus, the buildings of these states, with their wide porches and tall windows, seem more "Southern" than those of Virginia, the Carolinas and Georgia.

Rosemount, a few miles northwest of Forkland, Alabama, was built for the planter Williamson Allen Glover in stages between the mid-1830's and the 1850's. The principal front, with its two-story Ionic portico, probably dates from the early 1850's. The roof-top belvedere is more than a decoration, for it functions as a gigantic chimney to exhaust hot air up and out of the interior. Waverley, a unique design but another well suited to the climate, was built northwest of Columbus, Mississippi, about 1852 for George Hampton Young, a planter from Georgia. Shady, recessed Ionic

Rosemount, Williamson Allen Glover House, Forkland, Alabama, vicinity, c. 1835, enlarged in 1850's.

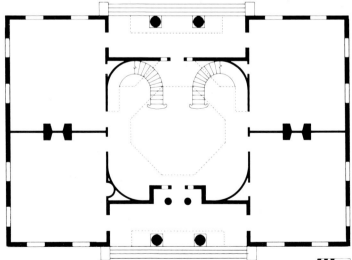

Waverley, George Hampton Young House, Columbus, Mississippi, vicinity, c. 1852, with
its plan.

Waverley, view of octagonal stair hall.

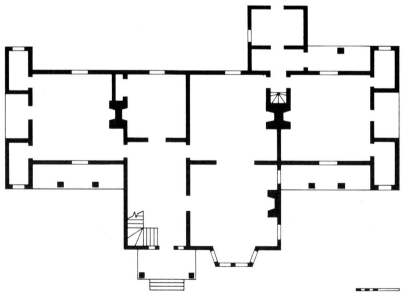

Westwood, Price Family House, Uniontown, Alabama, c. 1850, with its plan.

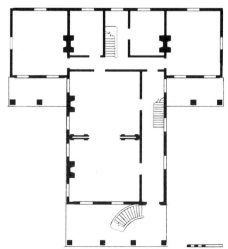

Oakleigh, James Roper House, 350 Oakleigh Place, Mobile, Alabama, 1833–38, enlarged in the 1850's, with its plan.

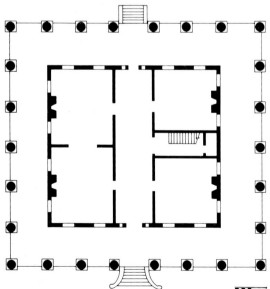

Dunleith, Charles Dahlgren House, Natchez, Mississippi, 1856–57, with its plan.

porticoes lead into an immense octagonal hall, sixty-five feet high, surrounded by balconies and stairs, which helps to cool the interior. The builder of Westwood, built in the 1850's outside the hamlet of Uniontown, Alabama, for the family of James Lewis Price, a planter-lawyer from Virginia, experimented with a sprawling plan enlivened by projecting corner pavilions and two-story end loggias that allow space for recessed cast-iron porches. Oakleigh, at 350 Oakleigh Place in Mobile, was begun for James Roper in 1833–38 and remodelled for Alfred F. Irwin in the 1850's. Oakleigh's T-shaped plan, with porches on the fronts of the wings as well as the center, provides maximum ventilation and shade. Waverley and Oakleigh are open to the public.

Surprisingly, considering the advantages of shade for all sides of a building in this climate, there were only four known houses with peripteral colonnades in these states—three in Mississippi and one in Alabama. Dunleith, originally called Routhland, was built at Natchez in 1856–57 for Charles Dahlgren, a banker-planter from Philadelphia. His builder, Maryland-born John Crothers, surrounded the mansion with twenty-six monumental Tuscan columns. Another builder from Maryland, a thirty-eight-year-old "master mechanic" named David Shroder, was the builder of another mansion surrounded by columns: Windsor, built for the rich planter Smith Coffee Daniell II, twelve miles south of Port Gibson. Windsor, now a haunting ruin, featured twenty-nine two-story-high cast-iron Corinthian columns.

Without academic training or opportunity for travel, the country carpenter had to depend on books for instruction and inspiration. These books illustrated designs for porticoes, doorways, window frames, stairs and chimneypieces, with solutions to complicated structural problems like stair and roof construction, and a handful of sample buildings. The Natchez booksellers Pearce and Bescancon offered "Lafeaver's, Benjamin's, Nicholson's & Shaw's Architects, Beauties of Architecture [and] Carpenter's Guide" in 1836.[48] These books of Minard Lafever, Asher Benjamin, Peter Nicholson and Edward Shaw, published in New York, Boston and Philadelphia, are another example of Northern influence upon the architecture of the Old South.

The most popular of all American architectural writers in the first half of the 19th century was the Massachusetts housewright Asher Benjamin. Perhaps because of his lack of sophisticated training, Benjamin featured strong, simple designs that became popular because they were easy to build. Born in Connecticut about 1773, Benjamin finally settled in Boston. Some forty-four editions of Benjamin's six books appeared before his death in 1845. The conservative Benjamin did not include Greek details

Plate 28 of Asher Benjamin's *Practical House Carpenter* (Boston, 1830). *Private Collection*

Top: The Burn, John P. Walworth House, 307 Oak Street, Natchez, Mississippi, 1836. *Private Collection.* Bottom: D. F. Alexander House, 803 West Commerce Street, Aberdeen, Mississippi, 1853. The front doorcases of both houses were copied from Benjamin's Plate 28.

in his books until the sixth edition of his *American Builder's Companion* in 1827, but three years later in his *Practical House Carpenter* he observed: "Since my last publication, the Roman School of architecture has been entirely changed for the Grecian." Plate 28 of *The Practical House Carpenter* was copied for the front door case at The Burn, home of Natchez mayor John P. Walworth, in 1836, probably by the builder T. J. Hoyt. The same design also appears at the Green G. Mobley House, Webster and Pearl streets, Gainesville, Alabama, c. 1845, and at the D. F. Alexander House, 803 West Commerce Street, Aberdeen, Mississippi, 1853.[49] Plate 28 of Benjamin's *Practice of Architecture*, published at Boston in 1833, was the source for the doorway at the Dr. William L. Cowan House, 441 East Barbour Street, Eufaula, Alabama, c. 1840. Plate 29 of the same work was copied for doorways of a medical office at Jacksonville, Alabama, c. 1840, and Ingleside, home of Scottish-born horticulturist Thomas Affleck, at the village of Washington, Mississippi, c. 1848.

Like Benjamin, Minard Lafever was sympathetic to the needs of self-taught country carpenters. Born at Morristown, New Jersey, in 1798, Lafever, like Benjamin, had been apprenticed as a carpenter and joiner. Lafever's designs were, however, more elegant than Benjamin's, and, because they were more complicated, they were used less often by country builders. We have already seen how Lafever's designs from his *Beauties of Modern Architecture* were used by William Nichols at the Mississippi Capitol and Governor's Mansion in Jackson. At the Capitol, doorways were taken from Lafever's Plate 26. At the Governor's Mansion, Corinthian capitals for the portico were taken from Plate 43, and, once again, doorways were taken from Plate 26. Lafever designs had also been copied by Stephen Decatur Button at the 1846–47 Alabama Capitol and were later employed at the 1850 Capitol in Montgomery. Button was probably the architect who copied Lafever's Plate 26 for interior doorways at the Pollard and Knox houses in Montgomery. The frontispiece of Lafever's *Modern Builder's Guide*—a Greek villa with a two-story portico flanked by one-story wings—suggested the form of Kenan Place, outside Selma, Alabama, c. 1845, and the Turner Thomason House, 704 South Main Street, Pontotoc, Mississippi, c. 1850. The Natchez builder Thomas Rose employed Lafever designs at Stanton Hall in 1857–59.

The greatest Greek Revival mansion of Alabama, Nathan Bryan Whitfield's Gaineswood, is located in a town that was given a Greek name, Demopolis, by a Frenchman who settled there in 1817. Whitfield, born in Lenoir County, North Carolina, moved to Alabama about 1835, at the age of thirty-six. In 1843 he purchased a two-room log structure that had been built about 1820 by George Gaines. In the next twenty years Whit-

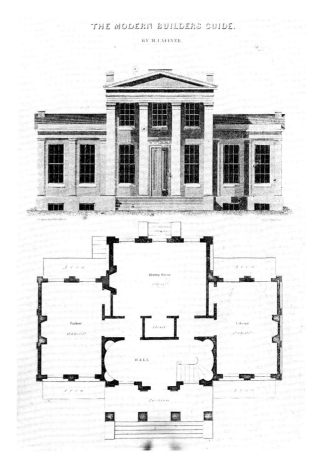

"Design for a Country Villa," frontispiece of Minard Lafever's *Modern Builder's Guide* (New York, 1833). *Private Collection*

Plates 28 and 29 of Asher Benjamin's *Practice of Architecture* (Boston, 1833). *Private Collection*

Dr. William L. Cowan House, 441 East Barbour Street, Eufaula, Alabama, c. 1840. Its doorcase was copied from Benjamin's Plate 28.

Ingleside, Thomas Affleck House, Washington, Mississippi, c. 1848. The doorcase was copied from Benjamin's Plate 29.

Kenan Place, Selma, Alabama, vicinity, c. 1845. *Photograph by Frances Benajmin Johnston, Library of Congress*

Turner Thomason House, 704 South Main Street, Pontotoc, Mississippi, c. 1850.

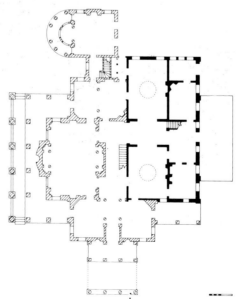

Gaineswood, Nathan Bryan Whitfield House, Demopolis, Alabama, 1843–60, with its plan showing enlargements.

field accumulated some seven thousand acres of land and nearly two hundred slaves. As a substantial planter with capital and skilled laborers, Whitfield sometimes acted as a builder of public works, including a plank road, a canal, an Episcopal church and agricultural fairgrounds. As his fortunes increased, Whitfield began enlarging and remodelling his house. The hall, library and dining room of the present house appear to be the oldest parts of a farmhouse transformed into a villa over the following twenty years.[50]

By 1847 and 1848 Whitfield had already begun his improvements. In February, 1848, he wrote to his son Needham: "I have not yet got my house inclosed, but hope to have it closed by the middle of summer, though I cannot hope to complete it before some time in the winter."[51] In early March, he wrote his cousin Rachel: "My house progresses very slowly and it seems as though I shall never get it inclosed. Mr. Rhodes [or Rose?] is still at work on it and I hope will get the roof all on in a few weeks at farthest. There is nothing done yet in the inside, though we are enabled to live in it quite comfortably."[52] Writing again to his son Needham about his house on March 21st, Whitfield added: "If you have heard great things of it you will be disappointed when you see it. I am merely adding to the old one and that, too, with such workmen as I can pick up about Demopolis, and they mostly negroes."[53] In October, Whitfield wrote to his son Bryan: "I am busied with my house, some 8 or 10 hands at work, and am now starting the outside which requires my particular attention."[54] In December, 1849, the house was being painted, and the first phase of expansion seems to have been completed by early 1850. Marble mantels from the shop of John Struthers at Philadelphia were shipped to Demopolis in 1853.

Ten years later, soon after Whitfield, long a widower, had remarried, he began enlarging his house for a second time, adding more rooms, new porticoes and a *porte-cochère*, making the western front into the principal entrance and enthusiastically embellishing the interior with details from Lafever's *Beauties of Modern Architecture*. Plate 19 was used for doorways, Plate 26 for decorations in the shallow domes into which large skylights were set, Plates 43 and 44 for capitals and the entablature of the ballroom, Plate 11 for the capitals in one of the new bedrooms and Plates 31 and 32 for capitals in another bedroom. In February, 1859, Whitfield wrote to his daughter Edith: "We have been the two past days engaged in tearing out the inside of the big room preparatory to finishing it, which I hope to do in the next three months, as I have a great deal of the work [cast plaster ornaments] already prepared to put up."[55] The frieze in the drawing room appears to have been taken from Plates 370 and 371 of *On*

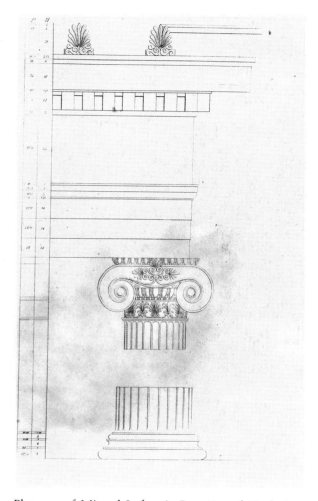

Plate 31 of Minard Lafever's *Beauties of Modern Architecture* (New York, 1835), used as a model at Gaineswood. *Private Collection*

Gaineswood, view of parlor.

Gaineswood, view of ballroom.

Gaineswood, view of a bedroom.

Gaineswood, view of bay window in second bedroom.

Gaineswood, in its original Romantic garden setting, engraving by John Sartain, c. 1860. *Alabama Historical Commission*

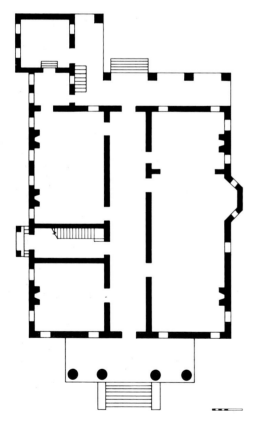

Plan of Stanton Hall.

the Use of Improved Papier-Mâché. . . . in the Interior Decoration of Buildings, published in London in the early 1840's by Charles Frederick Bielefeld, an English inventor and manufacturer of *papier-mâché* ornaments. In 1861 a new portico was added to the north front, and the old pantry was moved and replaced by a new bedroom with a circular gallery. In 1861 Whitfield wrote his cousin Rachel: "I have the house nearly complete, having just got through with the painting and papering. The parlor and dining room are also changed in effect by adding some lights to the ceiling which are very beautiful. The large drawing room is now completed and I think it is the most splendid room in Alabama."[56] Gaineswood is open to the public.

Gaineswood's asymmetrical plan and unexpected spatial vistas would have been applauded as "picturesque" by mid-19th-century architectural critics. Though Whitfield's whimsical agglomeration of rooms and details was created spontaneously as he tinkered with his house over a lifetime, Whitfield may also have been influenced by the coming of Romanticism to American architecture. The Greek Revival, which had been academic and rather severe in the 1830's and 1840's, was more and more often enriched with cast-iron and sawnwork inspired by a growing interest in Romantic design in the 1850's.

Romantic influence flavored the work of Natchez's veteran builder Thomas Rose. Born in England in 1806, Rose had come to Natchez in the late 1820's. Although Natchez never grew to spectacular size—its population was only 6600 in 1860—the city remained the social center of western Mississippi and northeastern Louisiana, with many rich families eager to display their wealth in fine buildings. In the mid to late 1850's Rose added stuccoed brick wings and cast-iron porches to Elms Court, a frame house built in the 1830's, for a Mississippi-born lawyer and diplomat, Ayres P. Merrill. The cast-iron porch at Elms Court, 142 feet long, is one of the outstanding examples of cast iron architecture in Mississippi.

In 1857 Frederick Stanton, an Irish-born cotton merchant, hired Thomas Rose to build a magnificent mansion on High Street. Stanton's probate papers state that Rose was paid for plans. The foreman was John A. Saunders, the masons Charles Reynolds from Pennsylvania and one Brown, the stucco-plasterers Price and Polkinghorne and the painter-grainer John Wells from England. Despite the Italianate character of its exterior, many details of Stanton Hall were copied from Lafever's *Beauties of Modern Architecture*, including portico capitals from Plate 11, doorways from Plate 19 and centerpieces from Plate 21. Stanton Hall is open to the public. Two other imposing mansions were built at Natchez in 1858: Magnolia Hall, erected for another cotton merchant, Thomas Henderson,

Stanton Hall, Frederick Stanton House, High Street, Natchez, Mississippi, 1827–28.

Stanton Hall, view of parlors.

Stanton Hall, doorcase in hall, with its model, Plate 19 of Minard Lafever's *Beauties of Modern Architecture* (New York, 1835). *Lafever illustration from private collection*

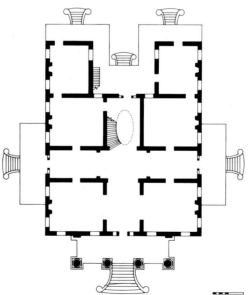

Homewood, David Balfour House, Natchez, Mississippi, vicinity, 1858, with its plan
and rear view of extensive porches, opposite. *Photographs from private collection*

Elms Court, Ayres P. Merrill House, Natchez, Mississippi, c. 1835, enlarged c. 1858.

Edgewood, Samuel H. Lambdin House, Natchez, Mississippi, vicinity, 1859.

Magnolia Hall, Thomas Henderson House, Natchez, Mississippi, 1858.

and Homewood, designed and built by James Hardie for the planter David Balfour. Magnolia Hall has been restored, but Homewood burned in 1940.

In 1859 Samuel H. Lambdin, a Pittsburgh-born merchant and extensive landowner, hired Thomas Rose to build his Greco-Italian villa, Edgewood, seven miles north of Natchez. Lambdin, who had worked his way from sailor to steamboat captain to a rich merchant, was one of those Yankees who became great Southerners. Edgewood was designed by two New Orleans architects, Henry Howard and Albert Diettel. Howard (1818–1884) was born at Cork, Ireland, the son of a local builder. He sailed to New York in 1836, worked in a picture-frame factory for eight months and then joined his brother in New Orleans in late 1837. There he was employed as a carpenter and stairbuilder for five years, studied for a time with James Dakin and opened his own architectural office about 1846.[57] Albert Diettel (1824–1896) was born in Dresden and worked as a mason and railroad engineer before coming to New Orleans by way of New York in 1849.[58] Howard and Diettel were partners between 1857 and 1860. The design of Edgewood combines Greek details—a trabeated entrance and one-story Corinthian portico—with others that are Italianate—wide bracketed eaves, a center gable and paired round-headed windows.

Aberdeen, on the Tombigbee River of Mississippi, was founded by the Scottish-born Indian trader and land speculator Robert Gordon from Nashville in 1836, but its importance as a trading center attracted a population of 5000 settlers by 1850. Of twenty-one carpenters in the county in 1850, none came from Mississippi; of nineteen brickmasons, only one came from Mississippi; of thirty-eight "mechanics" only one came from Mississippi. The Edward Herndon House, built at Aberdeen in the 1850's, was a conventional boxy building, but its daring builder used sawnwork brackets in place of triglyphs and metopes and substituted extraordinary sawnwork pillars in place of Greek columns, plus tiny pointed windows set in pairs. The Herndon House has been demolished. Also in Aberdeen is the Robert Adams House, now a masonic hall, on North Meridian Street, 1856, a conventional Greek Revival building of similar form and proportions.

Columbus, Mississippi, located at the intersection of the highway between Nashville and New Orleans, on the east bank of the Tombigbee River heading to Mobile, emerged as another market town of the northeastern counties. Vermont-born James S. Lull (c. 1814–1872) had come to Columbus by the early 1840's, when he served on a committee of the local mechanics society.[59] In 1846 Lull was paid $30 for a plan of the city hall; he designed and built a courthouse in 1847 (it was remodelled in

Robert Adams House, North Meridian Street, Aberdeen, Mississippi, 1856. *Library of Congress*

Edward Herndon House, Aberdeen, Mississippi, c. 1855. *Library of Congress*

Flynnwood, Columbus, Mississippi, undocumented, c. 1855. *Library of Congress*

Top: Malmaison, Greenwood Leflore House, Carroll County, Mississippi, c. 1852–54. *Library of Congress*. Bottom: Cowles Meade Vaiden House, Carroll County, Mississippi, c. 1855. *Library of Congress*

1901); and he probably built the imposing Riverview mansion for Maryland-born banker Charles McLaran about 1850. Lull is also believed to have been the builder of a distinctive group of large, boxy frame houses at Columbus that employed octagonal pillars, clustered columns and Gothic tracery in place of the usual details of Greek architecture. The grandest of these houses, Flynnwood, has been demolished and is undocumented. At Union Springs, Alabama, Dr. Stirling Foster House, 201 Kennon Street, 1852–56, is another boxy frame house enlivened by an unexpected Romantic detail—ogee arches spanning the spaces between the porch pillars.

Two similar mansions built in Carroll County, Mississippi, in the 1850's combined Greek forms with Italianate details. Malmaison, built about 1852–54 near Carrollton, was the home of Greenwood Leflore, the last chief of the Choctaw Indians. The son of a French trader, with an Indian grandmother, Leflore was educated in Tennessee, prospered as a large planter and served in the Mississippi legislature. According to tradition, Malmaison was built by Leflore's son-in-law, James Clark Harris (1826–1904) from Georgia. The same craftsmen almost certainly built the nearby Cowles Meade Vaiden House for a Carroll County planter-physician. These two designs featured two-story porticoes and balconies, with flush weatherboarding behind the porticoes, sawnwork brackets, balustraded roof decks and exuberant cupolas. Both houses have been destroyed.

Courtview, George Washington Foster House, on Court Street in Florence, Alabama, built in 1854–55 by a builder named John Ballinger, was ornamented with Italianate bracketed eaves; these have been removed by well-intentioned but misguided restorationists who did not appreciate the influence of Romanticism upon Classical design in the 1850's in Alabama. William Varner's Greco-Italian villa, Grey Columns, at Tuskegee is one of the largest 19th-century mansions of Alabama, Classical in form but featuring an octagonal belvidere, extensive use of cast iron and sawnwork eaves brackets. Rocky Hill, the summer home of James Edmunds Saunders, was built near Town Creek about 1858–61. James Saunders was a Virginia-born cotton merchant, the son of Turner Saunders who had built a Palladian house nearby in the 1830's. Though demolished in 1961, Rocky Hill can still be seen in photographs. The exterior featured two Doric porticoes, bay windows, bracketed cornice, an ornate cupola and a surprising, five-story, battlemented octagonal tower. The flamboyant interior woodwork, whose coarse opulence reflects changing sensibilities as much as rural isolation, has been attributed to the Welch-born carpenter Hugh Jones.

Courtview, George Washington Foster House, Court Street, Florence, Alabama, 1854–55. *Alabama Department of Archives and History, Montgomery, Alabama*

Grey Columns, William Varner House, Tuskegee, Alabama, c. 1855.

Rocky Hill, James Saunders House, Town Creek, Alabama, vicinity, c. 1858–61, exterior and parlor views. *Library of Congress*

Harvey Walter House, Holly Springs, Mississippi, c. 1860, featuring castellated octagonal ends and cast-iron lintels.

IV. *Romantic Styles*

Independent Protestant Chapel, Mobile, Alabama, 1822, detail from an 1824 map of the city by J. Goodwin and C. Haire. *University of South Alabama Archives*

Because of its association with the great cathedrals of the Middle Ages, Gothic architecture was often used for ecclesiastical building, especially by the Episcopalians and Catholics. In his *Essay on Gothic Architecture*, published in 1836, John Henry Hopkins, the Episcopal bishop of Vermont, described the transcendant association between Gothic design and Christian spirituality: "The multiple perpendicular lines of buttresses, crowned with pinnacles diminishing to a point, the mullioned windows, and the slender clustered pillars, lead the eye of the beholder upwards . . . in the sky . . . causing, by a kind of physical association, an impression of sublimity more exalted than any other sort of architecture can produce!" The earliest Gothic church in the states carved from the Mississippi Territory, the Independent Protestant Chapel at Mobile, was built in 1822, only three years after Alabama became a state. This small one-story frame structure with a crenellated roof, described in 1828 as "a neat, framed wooden building with a Gothic tower," was demolished after just thirteen years. The First Presbyterian Church, at Broad and Fourth streets in Tuscumbia, Alabama, was built in 1827–28. With its boxy shape and octagonal cupola, an oval panel inserted into the pediment and a modillion eaves cornice, this church was really a building more Classical than Romantic, despite the use of lancet windows. The interior of the First Presbyterian Church was remodelled in 1888, and additions were made to the exterior in 1923–24.

With the same eclectic and decorative spirit, pointed windows were features of the Federal-style, boxy, gable-roofed Masonic halls built at Huntsville, Alabama, in 1823 (demolished in 1918) and at nearby Athens three years later, in 1826 (demolished in 1968). With the revival of their brotherhood in England in the early 18th century, the Masons renewed the traditions of craft guilds, their membership favored the building trades and their halls often featured Gothic elements. It seems likely that the same builder would have created these two similar buildings. He is still unidentified but probably came from nearby Tennessee, the home of many builders who worked in northern Alabama.

First Presbyterian Church, Broad and Fourth streets,
Tuscumbia, Alabama, 1827–28.

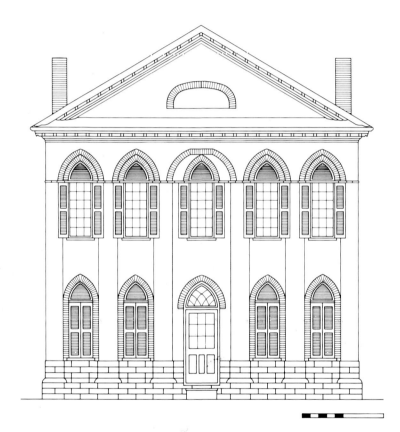

Masonic Hall, Athens, Alabama, 1826.

St. Mary's Chapel, Natchez, Mississippi, vicinity, c. 1837.

In Mississippi, both St. Mary's Chapel, built at Laurel Hill plantation twelve miles south of Natchez for planter-physician William Newton Mercer about 1837, and St. Mary's Catholic Cathedral, built in Natchez in 1842, were the work of master builder James Hardie.[1] Born in Scotland, Hardie (1807–1889) reached Mississippi by the mid–1830's. In December, 1837, he was appointed administrator for the estate of a carpenter named David McWatt. He worked as superintendent of construction for the builders Neibert and Gemmell. James's brothers Alexander, Robert, John and William were also carpenters. When Alexander died in 1839, his property included drawing instruments, mallets, planes and chisels. St. Mary's Chapel, intended for use by the Mercers and other families in the neighborhood, is a one-story stuccoed brick building with corner and side buttresses rising to slender finials, crenellations, drip-mouldings, a large Tudor-arch window under the gable and a delicate cast-iron bell tower. The principal embellishments to the interior are a communion rail carved with quatrefoils and black and white marble tiles paving the floor.

If St. Mary's Chapel is an exquisite jewel, then St. Mary's Cathedral is a Gothic behemoth. Its massive walls, as tall as a conventional four-story building, make a sweeping semicircular curve to form an apse at the Cathedral's east end. These walls appear even more commanding because they never received the stucco finish that the architect intended. When the cornerstone of the Cathedral was laid in 1842, Mississippi was already in the grip of a depression inaugurated by the Panic of 1837. Construction came to a halt in 1843, leaving the half-finished edifice with unplastered walls, rough floors, primitive furnishings and windows covered with boards, except for a single small pane of glass in each. Diocesan finances were so straitened that the Cathedral was put up for auction in 1847, though the bishop later withdrew it from sale. It was not until 1858–59 that Peter Warner, an Irish-born builder in Vicksburg, was hired to plaster the interior and lay floors. In the late 1850's, Warner built St. Paul's Episcopal Church at Vicksburg. Its rectilinear façade, with tall parapet walls, buttresses, crockets and central tower, recalls the design of St. Mary's Cathedral at Natchez.

Joseph Holt Ingraham, another of the New Englanders who came to western Mississippi and southern Alabama, was a popular writer of some eighty dime novels who later became an Episcopal priest. Born at Portland, Maine, in 1809, Ingraham came South in search of adventure about 1830 and remained to teach languages at Jefferson College, located at Washington, a village several miles north of Natchez.[2] After several years as a literary gadfly in New York and Washington, the national capital, Ingraham became a deacon of the Episcopal church in 1851 and was or-

St. Mary's Cathedral, Natchez, Mississippi, 1842.
Private Collection

St. John's Church, Aberdeen, Mississippi, 1853, an early view before renovations of the 1870's. *Private Collection*

dained to the priesthood the following year. In 1852 he was given charge of the newly established congregation at Aberdeen, Mississippi, where he supervised construction of St. John's Church, a modest Gothic church with a central entrance tower and crenellated parapet. In May, 1853, Ingraham reported to Bishop Green: "There being no church architect here who had any knowledge of Gothic construction, I was compelled not only to be the draughtsman but contractor and architect of the building, erecting it with the aid of two young men and nine slaves."[3] The two young men were Thomas Van Dozier, a North Carolina-born brickmason, and a carpenter named William Turner. They were also assisted by another brickmason named Thomas Brandon, who had a long and active career in Aberdeen. In the 1870's the original crenellated parapet of St. John's was removed when the roof was raised to correct a persistent leak. Ingraham died at Holly Springs, Mississippi, in 1860.

Throughout the antebellum period builders in Mississippi and Alabama added central towers, crenellated parapets, lancet windows, buttresses with weatherings and crocket finials to the traditional meeting house form that they had inherited from the 18th century. Christ Church, Vicksburg, was built in 1839–41. It survives, but with a disfiguring coat of coarse stucco. The first Church of the Nativity at Huntsville, Alabama, built by George Steele in 1847, was another gable-roofed, battlemented building with a projecting central entrance tower. Abandoned by the congregation when it moved to a new building in 1859, the first Church of the Nativity was finally demolished in 1878. The First Presbyterian Church, Adams Avenue, Montgomery, Alabama, was designed by Scottish-born Alexander McKenzie and built by John Poston Figh in 1847 and enlarged in 1859. St. Joseph's Catholic Church, 909 Church Street, Port Gibson, was begun in 1850 by Michael Foley of St. Louis but required several years to complete. St. Paul's Episcopal Church, Columbus, Mississippi, was designed by the obscure "Mr. Humpage" who had been sent from New York by the ecclesiastical architects Wills and Dudley to supervise construction of St. John's Church at Montgomery. Sometimes, as at the Fredonia Methodist Church, Como, Mississippi, 1848, and St. Mark's Episcopal Church, Raymond, Mississippi, 1854–55, lancet windows might be added as a gesture of religious symbolism to otherwise purely Greek Revival buildings.

Gothic design was also employed to symbolize military and academic as well as spiritual authority. The English-born William Nichols devised a Gothic-style penitentiary at Jackson, Mississippi, in 1836. Completed in 1840, this Penitentiary was demolished in 1901. Daniel Pratt, the pioneering industrialist from New England, had submitted a partly Gothic design

Christ Church, Vicksburg, Mississippi, 1839–41, a 19th-century photograph. *Old Courthouse Museum, Vicksburg*

Wesleyan University, Florence, Alabama, 1855.

for the rebuilding of the Alabama State Capitol at Montgomery in 1849, but his ideas were not adopted. In 1854 George Steele, the veteran Virginia-born builder of northern Alabama, enlarged and remodelled the Huntsville Female Seminary in the Gothic style.[4] Steele was then serving as a trustee of the Seminary. The institution had occupied a conventional gable-roofed Federal house at the corner of Randolph and Lincoln streets since 1836. Steele moved the entrance from Lincoln Street to the gable end that faced a garden on Randolph Street and added a crenellated parapet to the roof, so the gable became a kind of Gothic pediment over the new entrance. He also erected a new two-story wing with battlements, porches with lancet arches and an octagonal tower. The Seminary was demolished in 1912.

Adolphus Heiman, an architect and bridge builder from Nashville, designed two Gothic halls for Methodist colleges and a Presbyterian church in northern Alabama in the 1850's. Born in Prussia, Heiman (1809–1862) was the son of an official of the princely court. Trained as a stonecutter, Heiman came to America in 1834 and established himself in Tennessee by 1841.[5] The main hall of Wesleyan University, now the University of North Alabama, at Florence was built in 1855 by Zebulon Pike Morrison, a thirty-six-year-old builder from Virginia. This building is a symmetrical T-shaped structure with octagonal corner towers, battlements and a Tudor-arch entrance. Another Heiman design, Southern University at Greensboro, was built in 1857–59 by Andrew J. Mullen, a Massachusetts-born brickmason, and Robert Hall, a carpenter from Georgia, under the supervision of B. F. Parsons. Heiman's design included a projecting center tower, Tudor-arch entrance, buttresses with weatherings and crocket finials. After storm damage in 1973, the wrecked hall was taken down. Heiman also provided the design for the First Presbyterian Church, 312 Lincoln Street in Huntsville, in 1859. Its projecting corner tower was formerly surmounted by a 170-foot-high spire, which collapsed in 1878.

In the second quarter of the 19th century, church reformers in England sought to revive the Anglican liturgy by modelling new buildings in the style of medieval parish churches. These simple, solemn buildings were intended to fuse function and symbolism by representing in wood and stone a holier, less secular, kind of religious life, the theology and traditions of the ancient church cleansed of 18th-century rationalism and Classicism. In place of the boxy, light-filled churches of the 18th and early 19th centuries, these buildings would be darker, narrower, more mysterious. The New York Ecclesiological Society was founded in 1848 by anglophile church leaders to spread these concepts throughout America. The Society's journal, the *New York Ecclesiologist*, featured articles on church architecture, furnishings, music and ritual. In general, the Society advocated simple

Huntsville Female Seminary, Huntsville, Alabama, as Gothicized in 1854, detail from a map, c. 1860. *Map Division, Library of Congress*

Southern University, Greensboro, Alabama, 1857–59. *University of Alabama Library*

"Sketch of a First-pointed Church," in *New York Ecclesiologist*, October, 1849. *New York Public Library*

rather than elegant church designs. In particular, the Society specified the use of real materials, wood and stone instead of bricks and plaster, and provision for a separate chancel and the use of benches rather than pews. The English-born architect Frank Wills of New York, one of the handful of architects endorsed by the Ecclesiologists, wrote in his *Ancient Ecclesiastical Architecture* (New York, 1850): "As in morals, so in Architecture, honesty is the best policy. . . . Let us not be afraid of simplicity in building, and let us prefer a massive wall to a pretty moulding. . . . No house of God should be pretty."[6]

At first glance it may seem surprising to find so many Ecclesiologically "correct" anglophile churches in newly settled Mississippi and Alabama—indeed, many more than in the older and culturally more sophisticated states of the Upper South.[7] But it is not so surprising when we appreciate the two conservative bishops of the Episcopal church in antebellum Mississippi and Alabama who welcomed Ecclesiology. North Carolina-born William Mercer Green, the first bishop of Mississippi, who served from 1850 until after the Civil War, was described by his grandson as "an old-fashioned High Churchman." While serving as chaplain at the University of North Carolina in the early 1840's, Rev. Green had demonstrated his enthusiasm for architecture by leading the campaign to build an Episcopal church at Chapel Hill, obtaining a plan from Thomas U. Walter of Philadelphia and providing the bricks for its walls.

Soon after he reached Mississippi, the new bishop probably suggested the design for the Chapel of the Cross at Mannsdale (which was given the same name as Green's Chapel in North Carolina) to his friend, the rich North Carolina-born widow Margaret Johnstone, who wished to erect a church in honor of her deceased husband. The source of the design was a model church produced by Frank Wills and published in the *New York Ecclesiologist* in October, 1849. The builder, perhaps Jacob Larmour from New York, erected only the tall nave of the original design and omitted the tower and the transepts. Wills's design, with its wildly sloping roof and buttresses and bell-cote atop the west gable front, was unmistakably adapted from St. Michael's, a 12th-century stone church at Long Stanton, Cambridgeshire. Drawings of this particular building—one of three recommended models for small churches—had been sent across the Atlantic by the religious reformers in England. Thus, the Chapel of the Cross, consecrated in 1852, the first "correct" Gothic church in the states carved from the Mississippi Territory, traces its lineage, by way of the New York Ecclesiologists and Anglican church reformers, to a particular building from medieval England. A plantation tutor described the Chapel of the Cross in 1854: "Passing through the undulating grounds of the beautiful

Chapel of the Cross, Mannsdale, Mississippi, 1852.

Christ Church, Church Hill, Mississippi, 1857–58.
Library of Congress

park . . . you are in a path made through a dense forest tangled with great grape vines, enlivened by flocks of bright red birds. . . . After half a mile, you come to that gem of a church, standing in the grand solitude, upon a gentle elevation. You see . . . the light on the arched windows, and where it sharply defines each buttress."[8]

Other churches in Mississippi with features approved by the Ecclesiologists include St. John's Church, Glen Allan, Washington County, 1854–57; Christ Church, Church Hill, designed by J. Edward Smith of Natchez and built by N. L. Carpenter, 1857–58; and St. Peter's Church, 113 South 9th Street, Oxford, built by William Turner, a carpenter from North Carolina, 1857–58 with a steeple added in 1893. St. John's Church is now in ruins. Christ Church has the profile of its hammerbeam roof carved in relief on its stuccoed façade. The design of St. Peter's was probably influenced by Frederick A. P. Barnard, the Massachusetts-born professor at the University of Mississippi who was ordained an Episcopal priest in 1855 and then became the first rector of St. Peter's. Bishop William Mercer Green consecrated forty-one new churches in Mississippi during thirty years.

Nicholas Hammer Cobbs, from Bedford County, Virginia, served as bishop of Alabama from 1844 until his death in 1861.[9] Like Bishop Green, Cobbs was a conservative High Churchman, devoted to ritual, feast days and fasting. The bishop also served as rector of St. John's Church, 113 Madison Avenue, Montgomery, the first of three large brick churches in Alabama produced by Frank Wills and his partner Henry Dudley, two of the small number of architects endorsed by the New York Ecclesiologists.[10] Wills (1822–1856) had come to New York in 1847 by way of Canada and in 1851 formed a partnership with Henry Dudley (1813–1894), another Englishman whom he had known when they both worked in the office of the Devonshire architect John Hayward before coming to America. Copies of the specifications for building St. John's, Montgomery, are preserved at the Alabama Department of Archives and History. St. John's was built in 1853–55 under the supervision of an unidentified "Mr. Humpage" who had been sent to Montgomery from New York by Wills and Dudley. The builder was B. F. Randolph, a forty-one-year-old mechanic from Virginia.[11] Humpage also provided the drawings for St. Paul's Church at Columbus, Mississippi. St. John's was remodelled and enlarged in 1869 and 1879.

The second Alabama church by Wills and Dudley, Trinity Church, Mobile, was built at the corner of Jackson and Anthony streets in 1853–56. The spire shown in the architect's original design was not erected until 1884. In 1945 the church was taken down and rebuilt, without restuccoing

Christ Church, Church Hill, interior.

St. John's Church, 113 Madison Avenue, Montgomery, Alabama, 1853–55, a 19th-century view.
Alabama Department of Archives and History

Trinity Church, Mobile, Alabama, perspective view
by Wills and Dudley, 1853–56. *Trinity Church*

Church of the Nativity, Eustis and Green streets, Huntsville, Alabama, 1856–59, interior view.

St. John's Church, Mobile, Alabama, 1853, a 19th-century photograph. *Wilson Collection, Historic Mobile Preservation Society*

the walls, at a new location, 1900 Dauphin Street. The third Alabama church by Wills and Dudley was the Church of the Nativity, built in 1856–59 at Eustis and Green streets in Huntsville. Nativity's builder was Hugh N. Moore, a forty-six-year-old Virginia-born owner of a sash, door and blind factory. The exterior has been disfigured by harsh cleaning. Trinity and Nativity have similar interiors, which are two of the most beautiful in Alabama. In each, a dimly lit nave with low flanking side aisles is roofed by a series of trusses springing from a double row of wooden piers. Each truss terminates at the ridge in a delicate cusped trefoil. The arched side aisles also have traceried spandrels.

Another of the architects endorsed by the Ecclesiologists was Richard Upjohn of New York. Upjohn (1802–1878) had been trained as a cabinet-maker, surveyor and draftsman in England, travelled to America in 1829 at the age of twenty-seven and developed his skill while working in the office of the Boston architect Alexander Parris in the 1830's. Upjohn's design for the rebuilding of New York's Trinity Church in 1844 established his fame as an ecclesiastical architect and brought him requests for drawings from congregations throughout the land, especially those in areas of recent settlement where architects were unavailable and churches were poor. Fairly typical was a request from Rev. George Cushing, the Rhode Island-born rector of St. James Church, Eufaula, Alabama, who wrote Upjohn in August, 1850, asking for "a plain economical plan" for a church to seat 150–200 people.[12] "We are few and very feeble," Cushman apologized, "but we would give as much as we could rather than go on as others have done producing nondescript [churches]." Two years later Upjohn published *Rural Architecture*, a brief but enthusiastic guide for country carpenters containing sample plans for a cheap but substantial church, chapel, rectory and school house. In October, 1855, Thomas B. Bailey of Columbus, Mississippi, ordered a copy of *Rural Architecture*, because, he wrote the author, "I live in a part of the country destitute of that kind of knowledge."[13] Other copies of *Rural Architecture* were purchased by David Kerr of Jefferson County, Mississippi, and M. J. Conley of Montgomery, Alabama.[14]

For reasons not yet understood, Alabamians embraced the principles of *Rural Architecture* more enthusiastically than other Southerners. In his book, Upjohn explained how board-and-batten siding—boards laid vertically, their joints covered with thin slats or battens—could be used to produce inexpensive buildings that emphasized the verticality of the Gothic style. One of the first churches of this construction in Alabama was St. John's, Mobile, built in 1853 for a newly established congregation in a working class neighborhood in the southern part of the city.[15] The

Model country church from Richard Upjohn's *Rural Architecture* (New York, 1852). *New York Public Library*

St. Paul's Church, Lowndesboro, Alabama, 1856.
Library of Congress

cruciform plan may have been proposed by the energetic, peripetic Joseph Holt Ingraham, the first rector of St. John's. The builder-architect was David Cumming, son of a Scottish-born Mobile bookkeeper. The Church was enlarged, by widening the nave in 1854 and by lengthening the building in 1860, and demolished about 1956. David Cumming was also the builder of another board-and-batten church, St. Luke's, Cahaba, in 1852–54. In March, 1854, a local newspaper reported that St. Luke's had been built "after the designs of Upjohn, the celebrated architect, and published in his work upon rural churches."[16] In 1878 St. Luke's Church was moved to the village of Martin's Station.

Alabama produced more than a dozen board-and-batten churches before the Civil War. St. Andrew's, Prairieville, was built in 1853–54. The present entrance may replace a bell tower that was either never built or removed.[17] St. Luke's Church, 103 South Chinabee Avenue, Jacksonville, was built in 1856–57. T. A. Morris, the rector, wrote upon completion of his new sanctuary: "The principles of architecture, according to Upjohn's plan, have been strictly carried out, and this, we believe, is the reason why the edifice is so much admired for its harmonious order and its simple elegance and unpretending beauty."[18] Harmony, simplicity and honesty were the ideals of the Ecclesiologists. The plan of St. Luke's is nearly the exact mirror image of one of Upjohn's designs in *Rural Architecture*. St. Paul's Church, Lowndesboro, was built in 1857, with board-and-batten walls enriched with wooden buttresses, a projecting corner tower, a high, steeply pitched gable roof and lancet windows. St. John's-in-the-Wilderness was built in the Greensboro vicinity of Hale County in 1859 and moved to the village of Forkland in the 1870's.

While church reformers in New York broadcast Anglican prescriptions about the design of their buildings, new varieties of Romantic domestic architecture were also making their way to America from England by way of New York. In the 1850's Andrew Jackson Downing, the horticulturist and architectural theorist of Newburgh, New York, emerged as the principal tastemaker of mid-19th-century America. His books, *A Treatise on the Theory and Practice of Landscape Gardening*, 1841, which included an extensive discussion of rural architecture, *Cottage Residences*, 1842, and, most influential of all, *The Architecture of Country Houses*, 1850, provided inspiration as well as specific instruction for country builders. In these works, the formal, symmetrical houses of the early 19th century were replaced by informal, asymmetrical villas in Gothic and Italianate costume. Roofs became steeply pitched gables, with extended eaves and decorated bargeboards. Rooflines were further enlivened with clustered tall chimneystacks, towers, crenellated parapets, finials and crocket ornaments.

James A. Wemyss House, Greensboro, Alabama, vicinity, c. 1855. *Photograph by Frances Benjamin Johnston, Library of Congress*

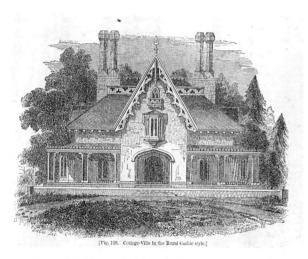

[Fig. 128. Cottage-Villa in the Rural Gothic style.]

"A Cottage-Villa in the Rural Gothic Style," Design XXIV from Andrew Jackson Downing's *Architecture of Country Houses* (New York, 1850). *Private Collection*

Façades were embellished with trellised verandahs, clustered columns, bay and oriel windows, Tudor and ogee and pointed arches, stone tracery and corner buttresses with weatherings. Instead of austere white, exteriors were painted warm earth tones. Interiors might be decorated with plaster vaults, leaded stained glass, drip mouldings and foliated ornament, but often the finish of rooms might be conventional and unadorned. A reflection of the Romantic movement throughout Western culture, these buildings were intended to be private, personal, sentimental and a little bit quirky. Influenced by the vast American landscape, which had so powerful an impact on painting and literature as well, Romantic architecture was intended to spring naturally, sympathetically, from its pastoral surroundings. Significantly, the Gothic Revival in America first flourished in the Hudson River Valley of New York, a center of landscape painting in the early 19th century. According to family tradition, the Gothic decorations—sawnwork bargeboards, pointed arches, trellised arcades and bays framed by interior ogee arches—were added to Robert Gracey's Waldwick at Gallion, Alabama, in the early 1850's after the owners returned from a trip to the Hudson River, where they had gone to escape the heat of summer and observed Romantic architecture firsthand.

Downing's works inspired several houses in Mississippi. The earliest of these was the rectory beside the Chapel of the Cross at Mannsdale, built about 1850, probably by the versatile Jacob Larmour of New York. A similar cottage, inspired by Design XXIV of *The Architecture of Country Houses*, was built in 1857 at 412 East Fortification Street in Jackson for Charles Manship, a Maryland-born decorative painter, carver and purveyor of paint and wallpaper who had come to Mississippi in the mid-1830's. Manship served as chairman of the building committee of the State Lunatic Asylum in 1850 and was mayor of Jackson during the Civil War. Manship's builders may have been W. W. Howell and W. A. Braselton, "architects and master builders" who listed Manship as one of their former customers in a newspaper advertisement. Manship House has been restored by the State of Mississippi and is open to the public.

Two even more exuberant Gothic houses were built at Holly Springs, a center for the processing and shipping of cotton in northern Mississippi. Cedarhurst at 490 East Salem Avenue was built for Pennsylvania-born Dr. Charles Bonner about 1857 and Airliewood at 385 East Salem Avenue was built for William Henry Coxe, a planter from Georgia, about 1858. The architect of these delightful buildings has not been identified. Although there is no specific evidence, he may have been Thomas Kelah Wharton (1814–1862), a designer with a demonstrated knack for the Gothic who lived in Holly Springs in 1844–45. Born in England, Wharton sailed to

Charles Manship House, 412 East Fortification Street, Jackson, Mississippi, 1857.

Cedarhurst, Dr. Charles Bonner House, 490 East Salem Avenue, Holly Springs, Mississippi, c. 1857.

Airliewood, William Henry Coxe House, 385 East Salem Avenue, Holly Springs, Mississippi, c. 1858.

John Calhoun Edwards House, 405 South 9th Street, Opelika, Alabama, c. 1860.

New York in 1830, worked in the office of the architect Martin Thompson and taught drawing at schools on Long Island. He taught school in Holly Springs in 1844–45 and then moved to New Orleans, where he resumed his career as an architect. There he was principal assistant supervisor of construction of the gigantic U.S. Custom House, by far the largest building of the era in the largest city of the region.

Horace King, a free black carpenter, was the probable builder of two Gothic houses at Opelika, Alabama, a new town on the railroad between Montgomery and Columbus, in the late 1850's or in 1865–66. Spring Villa, with its many, steeply-pitched gables, was built for William Penn Younge from Virginia seven miles south of the town. The John Calhoun Edwards House, 405 South 9th Street, was built for a Lee County planter. King, born a slave in South Carolina in 1807, had been brought to the Chattahoochee River Valley in the 1830's by his master, a bridge builder named John Godwin. Threatened with bankruptcy in 1846, Godwin emancipated King to prevent the misfortune of having his loyal bondsman sold against his will to pay debts. After a long and successful career as a house and bridge builder during the antebellum era (he helped build the Alabama Insane Hospital at Tuscaloosa in the 1850's), King became a political leader during Reconstruction. He died at LaGrange, Georgia, in 1887.

Of the Romantic styles, the Italianate became the most popular, primarily because it was easier to build than the Gothic and, with wide, overhanging eaves and long casement windows leading to shady loggias, seemed better suited to the Southern climate. The Italian Villa style was inspired by the rural architecture of the north Italian countryside and was often called the Tuscan style—for the province of Tuscany in northern Italy. Italian villas were generally asymmetrical in plan and massing, with a tall entrance tower, low roofs with wide eaves supported by sawnwork brackets, arcaded porches or loggias, and bay windows, and round-headed windows grouped in twos and threes, ornamented with heavy hood mouldings or pediments. Two large and characteristic Italian villas of the 1850's in Alabama have been demolished: Thomas H. Watts House at Montgomery and Gideon E. Nelson House at Greensboro.

Italianate additions to older buildings highlighted the characteristics of villa architecture that were most admired by Southern builders. The Huntsville, Alabama, druggist George W. Neal added an off-center tower, round-headed windows and bracketed eaves to his twenty-five-year-old house at 558 Franklin Street about 1850. Some five years later, John Drish, a physician-turned-builder of Tuscaloosa, added a projecting three-story entrance tower, bracketed eaves and cast-iron balconies to a conventional

Gideon E. Nelson House, Greensboro, Alabama, c. 1860. *Private Collection*

John Drish House, 2300 Seventeenth Street, Tuscaloosa, Alabama, as renovated c. 1855.
Photograph by Frances Benjamin Johnston, Library of Congress

Greek Revival house built about 1835. In 1860 the Natchez lawyer and amateur architect J. Edward Smith, who has also been credited with t' Greek Revival design of the Second Presbyterian Church at Natchez and the Gothic Revival design of the Episcopal Church at Church Hill, add a new Italianate front, featuring a two-tiered arcaded loggia flanked three-story towers, to W. C. Chamberlain's 1835 house on Myrtle Aven at Natchez.

Alexander Jackson Davis, the New York architect who had provide many designs that were published in the books of A. J. Downing, describe himself as an "architectural composer" and approached architecture as a artist rather than as a builder. Though Davis (1803–1892) was the partn of Ithiel Town for nearly ten years, off and on, Davis worked alone f most of his career, doing all his own drafting. He offered to provide architectural advice and drawings by mail to distant clients whom he knew only through letters. In December, 1855, and January, 1856, Davis sketched a design for a diminutive villa that was to be built at Columbus, Mississippi.[19] Davis never met the lady for whom the house was to be built or her brother, a farmer named Andrew Weir who lived outside Norfolk, Virginia, and ordered the drawings. Equally ironic was the source of the design: a house that Davis had devised seven years earlier for L. B. Brown of Rahway, New Jersey. Downing had published this design in his *Horticulturist* magazine in January, 1849, and also, the following year, in his book *The Architecture of Country Houses*. The villa intended for Mississippi was never built—the client did not like the design—but Davis provided similar drawings for a house that was built in Alamance County, North Carolina, and the published Davis-Downing design was copied for another house that was built at Franklin, Louisiana. Thus, a house at Rahway, New Jersey, spawned architectural offspring in North Carolina, Mississippi and Louisiana! This episode is another reflection of the national, not entirely regional, character of academic architecture in mid-19th-century America.

W. C. Chamberlain House, Myrtle Avenue, Natchez, Mississippi, as enlarged in 1860. Top: A view from Hinkle, Guild catalogue of 1862. Bottom: A current view, with third story of towers removed. *Catalogue illustration from the Collection of The Public Library of Cincinnati and Hamilton County*

Another New York architect who provided designs for Downing's books and also sold drawings to clients in distant regions by mail was Richard Upjohn. In April, 1851, J. H. de Bose of Liberty Hill, Dallas County, Alabama, wrote the architect for help with a house he was planning to build that fall. It was to be a "Country Villa" of frame construction, two stories high with a roof "as flat as may be," but it is not known what, if any, drawings Upjohn may have provided.[20] In January, 1854, Leonidas N. Walthall of Newbern, Greene County, Alabama, wrote to Upjohn in New York: "I propose to build me a dwelling House, and desire to avail myself of your great experience and highly cultivated Taste." One suspects that Walthall had seen a copy of Upjohn's *Rural Architecture* or knew his

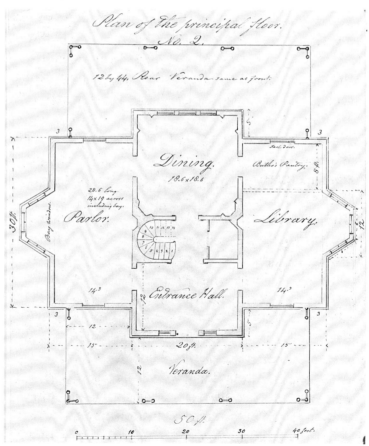

Design for a house to be built at Columbus, Mississippi, by Alexander Jackson Davis, 1855–56. *New-York Historical Society*

fame as a builder of churches, for he instructed Upjohn to make his house suitable for a "good Christian family." Walthall explained the number, types and arrangement of rooms he needed, including verandahs, large bay windows and wide halls. "The Pleasant breezes throughout our long, hot summers are generally from the south. It is therefore desired that the Chamber and dressing room (which rooms are more used than any others) shall be so situated as to get the full benefit of the south wind and that it shall pass unobstructed through them."[21] Walthall suggested that the Italian Villa style was "the one best suited to our climate." However, he finally asked Upjohn to copy the piazza and gables shown in Design XX, "A Villa Farm-House in the Bracketed Style," from Downing's *Architecture of Country Houses*.[22]

In October, 1857, after a three-year delay, Walthall wrote again, with apologies, to Upjohn. Walthall had not yet erected his house and would Upjohn provide more drawings?[23] This time, recognizing that he was dealing with an enthusiastic but indecisive client, Upjohn dispatched a long list of twenty-five detailed queries in November. After receiving replies, Upjohn provided two alternate schemes. In December, the final design — which included a "tower or look-out" and stained glass windows illustrating religious scenes — was approved. In February, 1858, William Hart, a New York carpenter selected by Upjohn, was sent to Alabama to supervise construction, assisted by several other workmen from the North, including men named Halliday, Ray, Davidson and Kemball. Meanwhile, blinds, sash, glass, hardware, nails, window weights, ovens, carpets and furniture were ordered from New York.

In May, 1858, William Hart in Alabama wrote to Upjohn in New York: "i like it [the South] well. i have a splendid mansion out here in the shape of a log house on the Place and fixed it up all right. i have 2 rooms 12 feet squar [sic] and will Build a small Cook Room. i Bought a good horse and Chickens. . . . i am getting quite settled. Some foulks talk about me Building them an other house allready but one at a time will suite me very well."[24] In June, the frame of Walthall's house was being raised and would soon be weatherboarded. In September, 1858, Hart again wrote to Upjohn: "i have had a hard job to carry out the Design. the[y] are very Changible p[e]ople here. What they think one day is nothing to do with tomorrow. . . . i tell him if he follows the Drawings in every respect he will have a good and convenient house."[25] Sash and glass had not yet arrived from New York, so Hart kept out the rain by hanging shutters to cover the window openings. In October, 1858, Walthall, who wanted to paint his house "a drab colour," a choice in accordance with Romantic taste for earthy, natural tones, sent his painter, one Winters, to New York to receive

"A Small Villa in the Classical Manner," Design XXIII of Andrew Jackson Downing's *Architecture of Country Houses* (New York, 1850), provided by Alexander Jackson Davis for a house in New Jersey and adapted for use in North Carolina, Mississippi, and Louisiana. *Private Collection*

Perspective view of Edward K. Carlisle House, attributed to Richard Upjohn, 1858. *Private Collection*

instructions from the architect. Walthall's house has been destroyed and its appearance is not known.

Meanwhile, Walthall shared his architectural enthusiasm with his brother-in-law Edward K. Carlisle, a Georgia-born cotton merchant from Mobile, and showed Carlisle the unused alternate drawing that Upjohn had submitted in November, 1857. In May, 1858, Carlisle asked Upjohn to turn these unused sketches into complete drawings for a house to be built near the county seat of Marion, Alabama. Drawings, suggestions, revised drawings, more suggestions and more drawings were exchanged in May and June. In July, Carlisle approved the final design, a large brick Italian villa with tower and front-facing gable of unequal height. The design recalls a similar villa created thirteen years earlier for Edward King at Newport, Rhode Island, which had been illustrated as Design XXVIII in Downing's *Architecture of Country Houses*. The architect's presentation view, discovered by the architectural historian Robert Gamble, has survived. William Hart, who was completing his work for Walthall, probably built Carlisle's mansion as well. Materials and fixtures, including brownstone trim, furnishings, carpets, curtains, floorcloths and velvet, were ordered from New York City.[26] The house seems to have been completed in early 1860. Another adaptation of Upjohn's design, copied from Downing's Design XXVIII, was built at Richmond, Virginia, in 1852.

Another request for mail-order architecture brought to Mississippi a building designed by Calvert Vaux, an English-born designer whom A. J. Downing had hired in London and brought to America in 1850. Vaux (1824–1895) worked with Downing at Newburgh on the Hudson River for two years. After Downing was killed in a steamboat explosion on the river he so loved, Vaux moved to New York City, opened an architectural office of his own and assisted Frederick Law Olmsted in the design of Central Park. In 1857 Vaux published his own book, *Villas and Cottages*. Two years later, Thomas E. D. Pegues, a planter and railroad investor of Oxford, Mississippi, asked Vaux to prepare drawings for a house. This villa was to be adapted from Design 27, "an Irregular Villa without Wing," in *Villas and Cottages*. Vaux had prepared that design for a client at Millville, Massachusetts, who planned to build it outside Middletown, Connecticut! An amazing treasure has survived—sixteen pages of drawings, including all four elevations, plans for the basement and chamber stories and many details, signed "C. Vaux, Architect, N.Y., 1859." Vaux's drawings provided for two baths with running water, a glazed conservatory and a wine cellar. The builder was William Turner, who had built St. Peter's Church, Oxford, in 1857–59. Pegues's villa, later given the name Ammadelle, was begun in 1859 and was not yet completed in 1861.

Edward K. Carlisle House, Marion, Alabama, 1858–60.

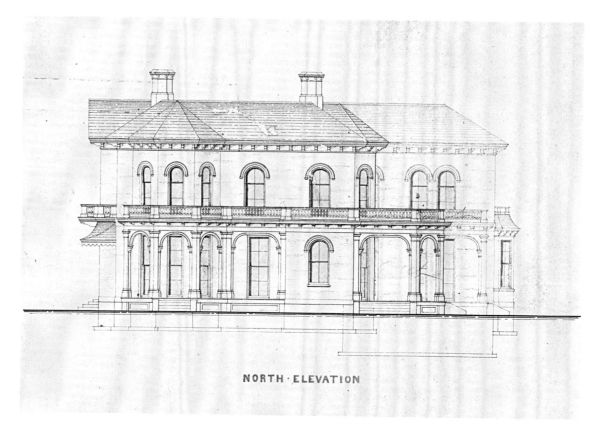

NORTH·ELEVATION

EAST·ELEVATION

Elevations for Thomas E. D. Pegues House, Oxford, Mississippi, by Calvert Vaux, 1859.
Private Collection

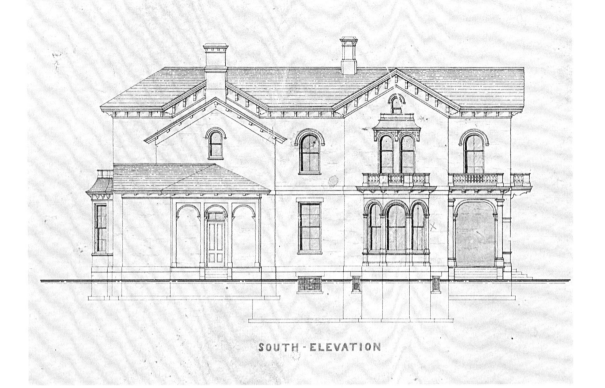

SOUTH-ELEVATION

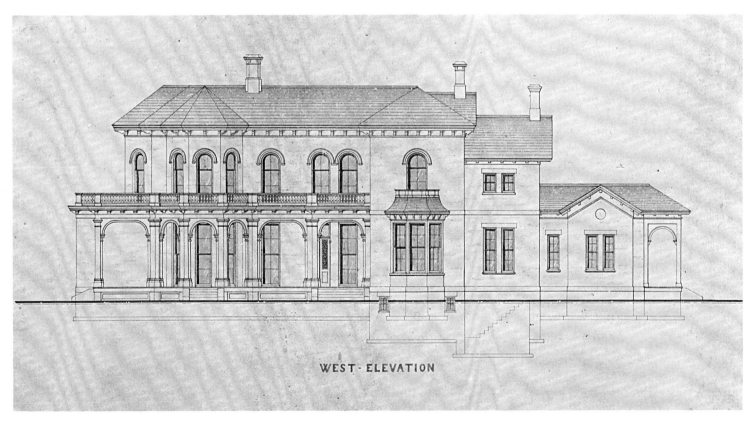

WEST-ELEVATION

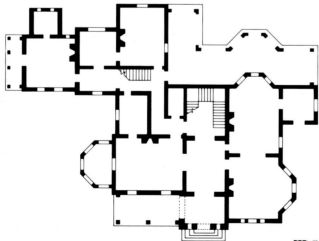

Thomas E. D. Pegues House, Oxford, Mississippi, 1859–61, with its plan.

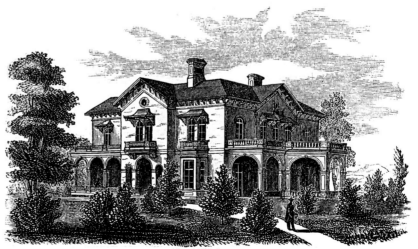

Mount Holly, Charles Wilkins Dudley House, Washington County, Mississippi, c. 1859–
60, with its model, Design 27 of Calvert Vaux's *Villas and Cottages* (New York, 1857).
Vaux illustration from private collection

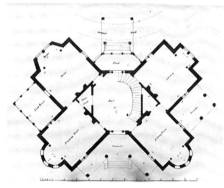

Design X, an "Anglo-Grecian Villa," from William H. Ranlett's *The Architect* (New York, 1847–49). *Private Collection*

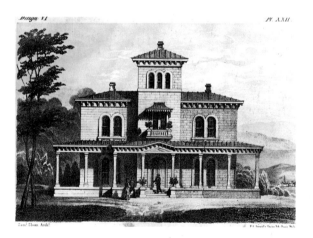

Design VI of Samuel Sloan's *The Model Architect* (Philadelphia, 1852–53), probable model for W. W. Topp House. *Private Collection*

Porches on the north side, window hoods and sawnwork brackets were not added until the 1890's. Vaux's Design 27 also reappears at Charles Wilkins Dudley's villa at Mount Holly in Washington County, Mississippi, c. 1859–60. The plan and elevation of Dudley's villa follow, in mirror image, Vaux's published design. The unidentified country builder misjudged the height of the walls and was obliged to eliminate the eaves cornice on which the sawnwork brackets should have been mounted.

We have often observed how important books were for the spread of architectural styles. The assortment of English books used by Levi Weeks at Natchez in the 1810's and the books of Asher Benjamin and Minard Lafever used by William Nichols and Stephen Decatur Button in the 1830's and 1840's had been illustrated dictionaries, containing pictures of the Classical orders, details of the capitals, columns and entablatures of ancient temples, with solutions to geometrical problems relating to construction of stairs, walls and roofs, a selection of designs for doors, windows, chimneypieces and mouldings, and a very small group of elevations and plans for sample houses and one or two churches. By the mid-19th century, authors and publishers had begun to create more elaborate books to serve the needs of an expanding architectural profession. These larger and more comprehensive works featured details, plans, perspective views and interior details for many model buildings in many styles—Greek, Gothic, Italian, Swiss and Oriental—and all were specific and complete with suggestions for landscaping, painting, furnishings, cost estimates and even philosophical essays on style.

Hiram Higgins, the veteran builder of Athens, Alabama, acknowledged the debt of the country architect to books when he advertised that he would provide "original *or copied* designs of all kinds of buildings . . . Grecian, Italian, Gothic, Tudor, Elizabethan, Oriental and Castilated."[27] The most popular mid-century pattern books were William H. Ranlett's *The Architect*, published at New York in 1847–49, and Samuel Sloan's *The Model Architect*, which appeared at Philadelphia in 1852–53. James S. Lull, the Vermont-born builder who was active at Columbus, Mississippi, in the second quarter of the 19th century, was the probable designer of two mansions copied from pattern books. The James Whitfield House, now known as Snowdoun, was built at 906 Third Avenue for a banker from Georgia in the 1850's. Its cruciform plan was adapted from Design X, an "Anglo-Grecian Villa," in Ranlett's *The Architect*. The W. W. Topp House, now known as Rosedale, was built about 1855 for a planter from Georgia. This villa, with its distinctive central tower, was copied from Design VI in Sloan's *The Model Architect*. Sloan's Design VI was also the source for two villas of the 1850's at Jacksonville, Alabama: Judge Thomas

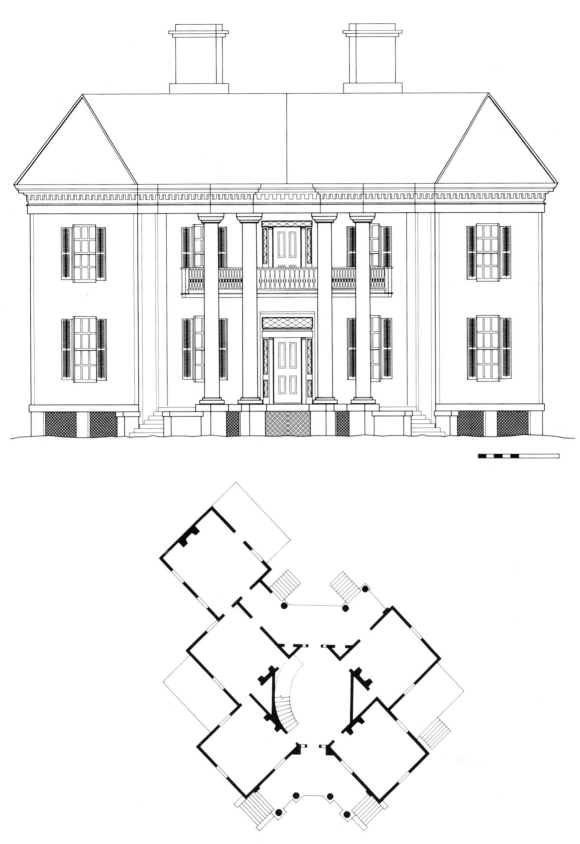

Snowdoun, James Whitfield House, 906 Third Avenue, Columbus, Mississippi, c. 1855,
restored elevation and plan by Mike Chapman.

Rosedale, W. W. Topp House, Columbus, Mississippi, c. 1855. *Library of Congress*

A. Walker's house, 601 North Pelham Road, and Ten Oaks, built for James Crook at 805 South Pelham Road by Elbert Morrison, a mechanic from North Carolina.

Another builder with books was Jacob Larmour (or Lamour), who worked in Canton, Mississippi, between 1850 and 1859. Born in New Jersey about 1823, Larmour worked in New York City between 1844 and 1850. He was probably sent to Mississippi to build the Chapel of the Cross at Mannsdale, copied from an illustration in the *New York Ecclesiologist*, and its nearby parsonage, a small Gothic cottage, inspired by Downing's *Architecture of Country Houses*. In 1853 Larmour built Grace Church, a board-and-batten frame structure, and its adjoining parsonage at Canton.[28] In the same year he began construction of the Odd Fellows Hall at Canton, completed two years later with the assistance of brickmason David Dean, who had come to Mississippi from North Carolina by way of Tennessee.[29] Larmour also designed the Baptist Church-College Chapel at Clinton, a temple-form building copied from Design XXXV of Sloan's *The Model Architect*. Larmour may have been the unidentified builder who added a new front to David Fulton's house at 239 East Center Street, Canton, in the 1850's. Fulton, an early settler from Maryland who prospered and became an influential state legislator, had built his house about 1830. The new façade, with its three-story central tower flanked by front-facing two-story gables, was copied from Sloan's Design I, with the porch and second-story window copied from Sloan's Design VI. Sloan's Design VI was also the source—and Larmour the possible builder—of Bellevue, an Italian villa built nine miles west of Canton for Benjamin Ricks about 1850–52. In an 1854 newspaper advertisement Larmour offered to draw plans in the "Swiss, Italian, Elizabethan, Norman and Old English styles."[30]

Larmour's masterwork was Annandale, an Italianate mansion in Madison County outside Mannsdale, erected for the rich widow Margaret Johnstone in 1857–59. Its design was adapted from Villa IV in Minard Lafever's *Architectural Instructor* (New York, 1856), a boxy villa intended by the author to be built at a country seat in the Middle or Southern states. With his final book, Lafever abandoned the Greek Revival designs and modest format of his earlier works and replaced them with lavish Romantic designs presented in elaborate detail. Mrs. Johnstone was probably attracted by the design's ample arcaded porches and spacious halls, which afforded abundant shade and ventilation, as well as by the design's massive grandeur. In September, 1857, Henry Sansom, rector of the nearby Chapel of the Cross, wrote that Mrs. Johnstone's "new house is under way but [the] frame not yet up."[31] The house at Annandale burned in 1924.

Design I of Samuel Sloan's *The Model Architect*, probable model for additions to David Fulton House, Canton, Mississippi, c. 1855. *Private Collection*

Villa IV of Minard Lafever's *Architectural Instructor* (New York, 1856), the model for Annandale, Margaret Johnstone's villa in Madison County, Mississippi, 1857–59. *Private Collection*

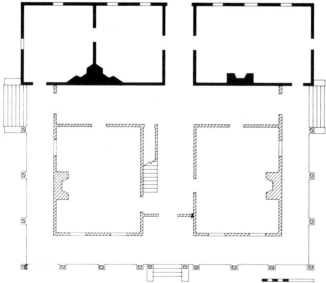

David Fulton House, 239 East Center Street, Canton, Mississippi, c. 1830, as enlarged
c. 1855, with its plan.

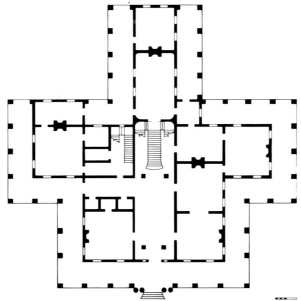

Annandale, Margaret Johnstone House, Madison County, Mississippi, 1857–59, as photographed before 1924 fire, with its plan. *Photograph from Mississippi Department of Archives and History*

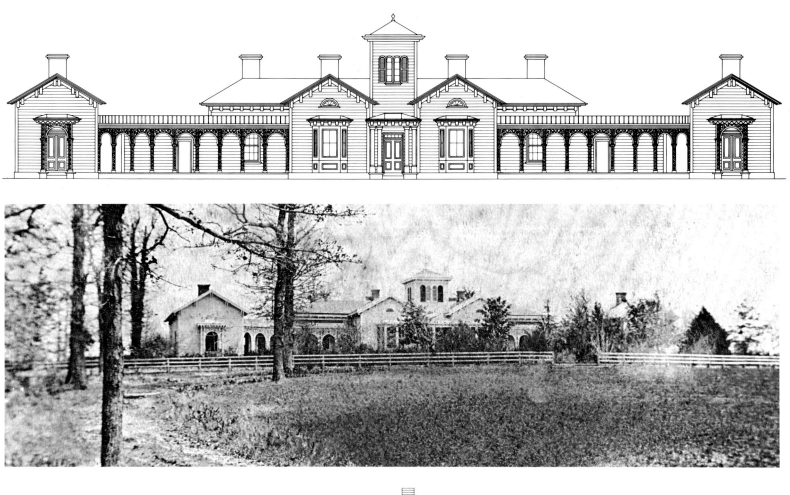

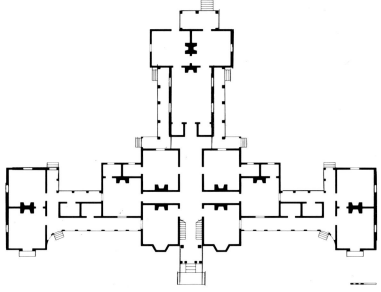

Ingleside, William J. Britton House, Pocahontas, Mississippi, vicinity, c. 1860, photo-graph prior to 1905 fire, restored elevation and plan. *Private Collection*

Nearby, the sprawling Italian villa at Ingleside plantation, outside Pocahontas, Mississippi, was built in the late 1850's for Mrs. Johnstone's son-in-law, the planter-merchant William J. Britton from North Carolina. Documentation has not been located, but one suspects that Jacob Larmour, who enjoyed Johnstone family patronage, was the builder. The central block, with its tall central tower flanked by front-facing gables, was inspired by Sloan's Design I, and sawnwork details for the porches and arcaded passageways were copied from Sloan's Design XXXII. The curving passageways leading to advanced dependencies are a grand, though by this time very antiquated, reflection of 18th-century Palladianism. One surviving family photograph suggests the splendor of the interior, with fancifully painted walls and stenciled floorcloths. The house at Ingleside, described by a plantation tutor of the 1850's as "the most elegant establishment I've ever seen in the South," burned about 1905.

In August, 1859, Larmour and his wife Elizabeth sold their property in Canton and moved to Hinds County, where they were living at the time of the 1860 census. Larmour built Tugaloo Mansion on the northern outskirts of Jackson about 1860 for John W. Boddie, a planter from North Carolina who was probably a friend of Mrs. Johnstone and William Britton, also from North Carolina, in this relatively small society of influential planters. Neglected and unappreciated, Tugaloo Mansion is now used as offices for a small college. Larmour's subsequent career has not yet been uncovered.

Prefabricated parts for Tugaloo Mansion and other villas by Larmour were supplied by Hinkle, Guild and Company of Cincinnati, manufacturers of panel doors, sash, blinds, window and door frames, mouldings, bases, pilasters, weather-boarding, flooring, shelving, lumber and ready-made houses. Hinkle, Guild products were distributed to builders up and down the Mississippi River. In 1853 the Hinkle, Guild agent in Natchez was a Pennsylvania-born merchant named A. L. Wilson.[32] Two other little-known Mississippi builders also used materials supplied by Hinkle, Guild. Arthur Doyle, born in Ireland about 1820, designed at least three Italian villas at Lexington, where he also served as an early mayor. All three of these buildings have burned, as well as the courthouse with its records, so the Hinkle, Guild catalogue is our source of knowledge for these works. Robert Tratt, born in New York about 1836, was a carpenter who lived in a rooming house at Fayette, Mississippi, with another New York-born carpenter named Benjamin Slowman. Tratt produced an Italianate house for Abner Kennison of nearby Franklin County. Its builder was a young master mechanic from England named John Manifold, who used materials manufactured by Hinkle, Guild.

Tugaloo Mansion, John W. Boddie House, Jackson, Mississippi, 1860, illustrated in the Hinkle, Guild catalogue of 1862 and seen in a photograph c. 1890. *From the Collection of The Public Library of Cincinnati and Hamilton County, Mississippi Department of Archives and History*

Mrs. Eggleston House and Rev. W. Holman House, Lexington, Mississippi, c. 1860, illustrated in 1862 Hinkle, Guild catalogue. *From the Collection of The Public Library of Cincinnati and Hamilton County*

Lithographed elevation of the Custom House, Mobile, by Ammi B. Young, 1852. *Mobile Public Library*

Despite the South's reputed antipathy to industry, prefabrication had a long and honorable history in the states carved from the Mississippi Territory. In 1801 Peter Little, a settler from Pennsylvania, moved to Natchez and set up a sawmill powered by the first steam engine brought into the Territory. In 1817 Stephen Hallet from New York shipped house frames, with a group of Northern carpenters to assemble them, to Mobile. In the 1830's house frames from Pennsylvania were shipped down the Mississippi River to Natchez. The elaborate ornament in wood and metal, so necessary for Romantic architecture, was facilitated by sawmills and foundries. Many master builders, including Andrew Brown and the Weldon brothers of Natchez, Hugh Moore of Huntsville and Barachias Holt of Montgomery, operated sawmills.

In the late 1840's manufacturers discovered that cast iron was stronger, lighter and cheaper than brick and also allowed more light and ventilation. Cast iron for the Mississippi Insane Asylum was supplied by Jabez Reynolds of Cincinnati in 1854–55. The façade of the Central Bank at 1 Dexter Avenue in Montgomery, Alabama, features cast-iron decorations from Philadelphia, the home of its designer, Stephen Decatur Button. The cast-iron façade of the Daniels, Elgin Company Store at 51 Dauphin Street in Mobile, and other commercial buildings in the port, were produced by Daniel Badger, a Massachusetts-born manufacturer of cast iron in New York City.[33] The veteran builder Thomas Rose of Natchez installed splendid Corinthian columns of cast iron on the portico at Stanton Hall and erected a remarkable 142-foot-long cast-iron porch at Elms Court, the home of Ayres P. Merrill, a Mississippi-born lawyer and diplomat. The streets of Mobile were once lined with boxy brick houses shaded by cast-iron galleries. The twenty-nine cast-iron Corinthian columns of Windsor, the great ruined mansion south of Port Gibson, Mississippi, were made in St. Louis.

Mass production was taken a step further by the national government in the 1850's. Ammi B. Young (1800–1874), the son of a builder-architect, was born in New Hampshire. After working in Vermont and Massachusetts in the 1830's and 1840's, he succeeded Robert Mills as supervising architect of Federal buildings in 1851. Under Young's direction, the new Construction Branch of the Treasury centralized the design and construction of government buildings throughout the nation. Young created standard designs for buildings, many of them in the Renaissance Revival style, adapted from 15th-century Italian palaces, a dignified but relatively plain style that could be easily modified. Sheets of lithographed plans, elevations and details were published for buildings of the same type and size, sometimes merely substituting new place names on otherwise identical plates

Custom House, Mobile, Alabama, 1852–54. *Wilson Collection, Historic Mobile Preservation Society*

before issuing orders for similar projects in different cities. One design was used in ten different cities. The Mobile Custom House of 1852–54 has its parallels in Ohio, Vermont, Illinois, Iowa and Michigan. The builder of the Custom House at Mobile was Charles C. Ordeman, a young German engineer who had worked as city engineer at Montgomery in the early 1850's and designed the Montgomery Courthouse of 1854.[34] The Custom House at Mobile was demolished in 1963.

Italian architecture was adapted to an entirely new building type at the Alabama Insane Hospital, built over an extended period between 1852 and 1861.[35] In 1852 the Alabama legislature had authorized construction of a state hospital for the insane and dispatched a building committee to inspect institutions in the Northern states. Dr. Thomas Kirkbride, chief physician of Philadelphia's Hospital for the Insane and a tireless advocate of compassionate care for the mentally ill, offered this committee his inspirational ideas about hospital design. The State of Mississippi had already begun construction of a mental hospital at Jackson that featured many of Dr. Kirkbride's concepts. Kirkbride believed that everything in an ideal mental hospital should offer an inviting and cheerful environment for healing. A beautiful, pastoral setting would provide a calm background, and the forbidding walls necessary to keep patients in and strangers out of the hospital grounds could be hidden from view by erecting them in deep trenches. Sprawling wings would offer views of the landscape and allow decentralization. Thoughtful provision for heating, ventilation, running water and fresh food would further improve general conditions. Attention to small details—the design of windows that minimized security requirements—would contribute to the restorative environment.[36]

Kirkbride also recommended an architect to build that ideal mental hospital in Alabama—the young Samuel Sloan. Born in Pennsylvania in 1815, Sloan had been apprenticed to a carpenter and cabinetmaker before beginning the customary advancement from craftsman to builder to architect. Kirkbride had met Sloan when Sloan was supervising construction of the Pennsylvania Hospital in 1840–41. Though the bulk of Sloan's work was concentrated in the Philadelphia area, Kirkbride's endorsement helped Sloan become one of the most prolific hospital designers of 19th-century America. The Alabama Insane Hospital was the first of thirty-two hospitals that Sloan would design during his long career. In 1883, Sloan added wings to Robert Mills's State Hospital at Columbia, South Carolina, and Sloan died in 1884 at Morganton, North Carolina, where he was supervising construction of the Western North Carolina Insane Asylum.

Sloan's design for the Alabama Insane Hospital provided for a four-story brick building with offices, chapel, parlors, staff quarters, kitchens and

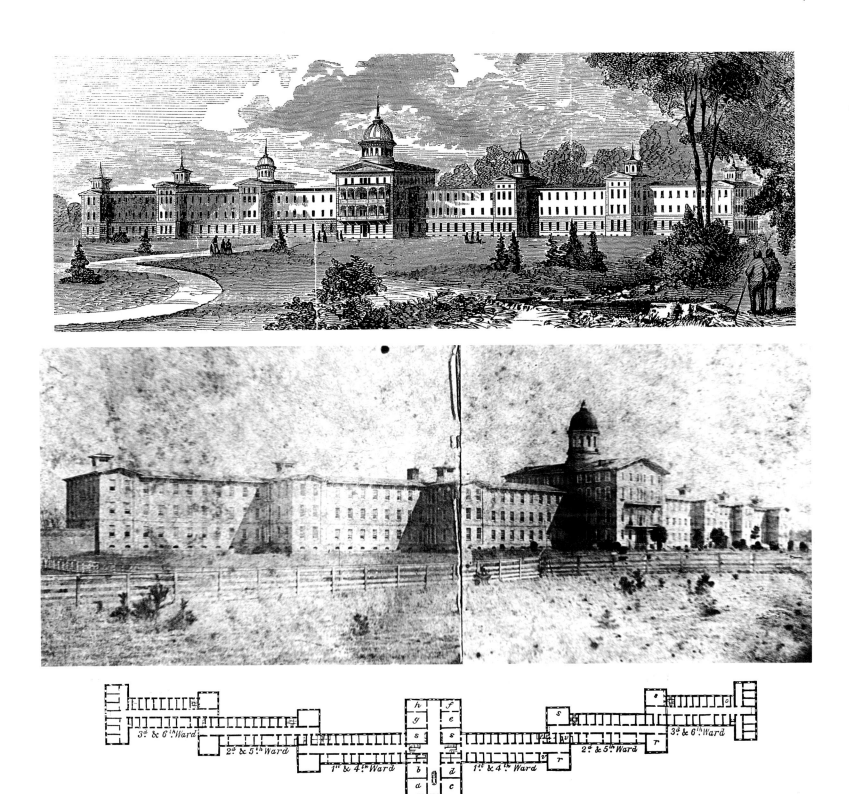

Insane Hospital, Tuscaloosa, Alabama, 1852–61, an early photograph, with a perspective view and plan from Thomas Kirkbride's 1854 book on mental hospitals. *Photograph from University of Alabama, Kirkbride illustrations from New York Public Library*

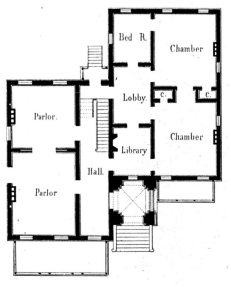

Design LIII, "A Southern House," from Samuel Sloan's *The Model Architect* (Philadelphia, 1852–53). *Private Collection*

storerooms, adorned with a cast-iron portico and surmounted by a copper-clad dome. Sprawling wings, spanning 784 feet, were arranged as pavilions with hyphens in receding planes, containing rooms for three hundred patients, men in the west wing and women in the east wing. Heat was provided by steam pipes, and ventilation was facilitated by fans. Twenty-one bath tubs and cast-iron water closets were to be supplied with hot and cold running water. There were also provisions for speaking tubes, gas lights, dumb waiters and a miniature railroad in the basement for food delivery.[37]

Construction of the Alabama Hospital began in 1853 on a site two miles east of Tuscaloosa near the University. The work was supervised until 1857 by John Stewart, Samuel Sloan's partner between 1852 and 1857, then by Samuel Sloan's young half-brother Fletcher Sloan (1826–1883) and finally by Alexander Anderson, also from Pennsylvania.[38] Brickwork was undertaken by William D. Robinson, and the painting and glazing was by Charles T. Moore. Carpentry was provided by Fletcher Sloan and his partner Robert Jemison, Jr., a Georgia-born lawyer and investor in stage coach lines, coal mines, plank roads and lumber mills. As a state legislator, Jemison had been the most insistent advocate for building the Insane Hospital and then used his political influence to obtain contracts for the lumber, cast iron and carpentry at the Hospital for himself and his partner in the building business. After several years of delay, Jemison complained that Fletcher Sloan was unable to keep financial records and worked as slowly as "a Terapin [sic] in a thunder-storm."[39] Finally, the exasperated Jemison demanded an end to the partnership, and additional work at the Hospital was supplied by another associate of Jemison, the free black carpenter Horace King. The Alabama Insane Hospital opened in July, 1861, though the east wing was still unfinished and the elaborate mechanical systems ordered from Philadelphia were never delivered.

While the Sloan brothers and Stewart were so often in Alabama, they were employed to provide drawings for other buildings in the area. Samuel Sloan featured the design of the Joseph Winter House in Montgomery, now demolished, in the second volume of *The Model Architect*. We do not know precisely when Sloan designed this Italian villa for a Georgia-born lawyer, but it may have been as late as 1852–53, for, although the first volume of Sloan's book appeared in 1852, the second was not issued until 1853. Sloan intended that this "Southern House" would accommodate the hot climate by providing a detached kitchen, large windows, wide doors, ample verandahs and hollow walls. The Winter house was demolished about 1920. Sloan was active in the South, and, with luck, more of his Southern work will be identified in the future.

Joseph Winter House, Montgomery, Alabama, c. 1852. *Alabama Department of Archives and History, Montgomery, Alabama*

Robert Jemison House, 1305 Greensboro Avenue, Tuscaloosa, Alabama, 1859–62.

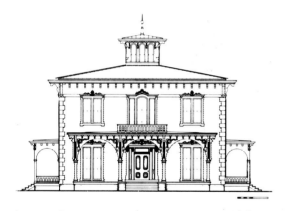

John B. Garrett House, Montgomery, Alabama, 1860.

In March, 1854, John Stewart announced that, because he was then "engaged in work in Alabama which would require his personal supervision for a number of years," he was ready to design and supervise construction of buildings throughout Alabama.[40] Stewart's design for Tuskegee Female College, built in 1855–56 and burned in 1912, featured a Tudor-arch entrance, two-stage battlemented tower, stained glass, drip mouldings and projecting octagonal corner turrets.[41] Four years later Stewart provided the design of a house in Tuscaloosa for Fletcher Sloan's partner, Robert Jemison, Jr., whose family had come from Philadelphia.[42] This work was supervised by a carpenter from Philadelphia named Lewis.[43] The brickmason was William D. Robinson. In early August, 1859, Jemison wrote Stewart that Robinson had not yet commenced the brickwork, but that Lewis had already prepared the frame for the wooden servants' house and for the main house. By the end of the month, excavations for the foundation were nearly complete, Robinson was beginning the brickwork and Lewis was preparing door frames. In March, 1860, work was delayed by a shortage of brick and a disagreement between Robinson and Jemison. When Jemison complained that Lewis was slow and old fashioned, Stewart replied that Lewis would get into no difficulties if he simply followed the drawings.[44]

Meanwhile, Orson Squire Fowler had published his book *A Home for All, or the Gravel Wall and Octagon Mode of Building* in 1848, single-handedly popularizing a new architectural fad. Fowler (1809–1887) was a phrenologist, vegetarian, teetotaler, sex educator and publisher whose exotic, quixotic architectural ideas appealed to the emotional and idealistic age in which he lived. Fowler claimed that his concepts had been inspired by the natural world. Like Nature's own favorite shapes—fruits, eggs, nuts, seeds and tree trunks—Fowler believed that houses should be circular or, next best, octagonal in plan. Fowler promised that octagonal buildings would be "several hundred percent" cheaper than others, because they enclosed more space within smaller walls. Similarly, these walls should be erected with Nature's own building materials—lime, stone and sand—which would be "simple, durable, easily applied, everywhere abundant, easily rendered beautiful, comfortable and every way complete."

Although octagons were never a great favorite in the South, at least two examples were produced in Alabama. The James Lane House at Athens was a two-story frame building with two, two-story square-pillared porticoes, built for a farmer from Georgia about 1854. The Lane House was demolished in 1953. The B. F. Petty House near the square in Clayton was built for a carriage-maker from New York about 1860. Its design was copied from "The Best Plan Yet," which appeared at the end of Fowler's

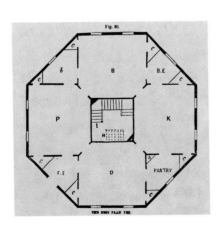

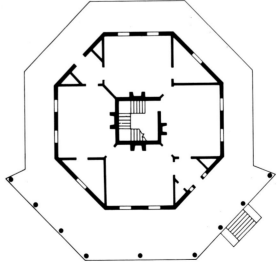

B. F. Petty House, Clayton, Alabama, c. 1860, with "The Best Plan Yet" from O. S. Fowler's *A Home for All* (New York, 1848) and the plan of Petty House. *Fowler illustration from private collection*

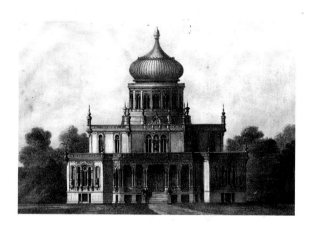

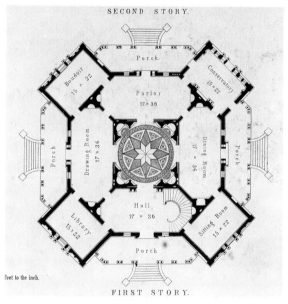

SECOND STORY.

FIRST STORY.

feet to the inch.

Design XLIX, "An Oriental Villa," from Samuel Sloan's *The Model Architect. Private Collection*

book, and its "gravel wall construction" follows Fowler's instructions for making a concrete-like mixture of lime and stones. Two octagonal houses were also built in Mississippi. One of them was built for Dr. William Nathaniel Raines in Desoto County about 1860. Its plan was copied from John T. Brown's house at Williamsburg, New York, published in *A Home for All*, and also adopted Fowler's ideas for board-wall construction, or horizontal boards used in place of the diagonal braces of timber framing.

Longwood, the largest and most spectacular octagonal house in America, was designed by Samuel Sloan for Haller Nutt, a Mississippi-born planter-physician who enjoyed an independent income from 43,000 acres on twenty-one plantations worked by eight hundred slaves. Nutt owned a copy of Sloan's *Model Architect*, in which the architect had published an octagonal "Oriental Villa." One suspects that Sloan probably included this fantastic, grandiose and impractical design in the book merely to demonstrate his virtuosity, and he must have been surprised when a rich Mississippi panjandrum asked him to design a *larger* version of it! Sloan made two trips to Natchez in January and May, 1860, to discuss the plans and lay out the foundations. In February, bricks were being made on the site. In March, Nutt's workmen—fifteen men and eight boys—were tearing down the old house on the property and excavating for the foundations. This gigantic structure required some 120,000 feet of lumber and 80,000 feet of lathing, which were prepared by Andrew Brown's sawmill in Natchez. Window frames, doors, sash, sawnwork brackets, blinds, columns, nails, tin, slate, lime, marble mantels, sills and chimney caps were sent from Philadelphia.[45]

In March, 1860, Samuel Sloan's plans were completed, and in April, Addison Hutton, a carpenter from Philadelphia who had been working on two Sloan churches at Wilmington, North Carolina, was sent to supervise the work at Natchez. Hutton (1834–1916) was born in Westmoreland County, Pennsylvania, the son of a village carpenter. He had worked as a carpenter and school teacher and learned about architecture and drawing during his employment at a sash and door factory in Salem, Ohio. He worked as a draftsman in Sloan's office in Philadelphia in 1857–61 and as Sloan's partner in 1864–68 and became one of Philadelphia's principal architects in the late 19th century.[46]

In March, 1861, the four bricklayers from Philadelphia—Charles Porter, Peter Willets, William L. Room and Oliver Schwarz—completed their work and returned to the North. In May, Nutt wrote Sloan that the roof was ready for the tinners: "The finish is all painted, sanded, and up; the Dome complete—brackets all up except in the lower cornice and most of the cornice complete to all the upper parts. It is creating much admiration

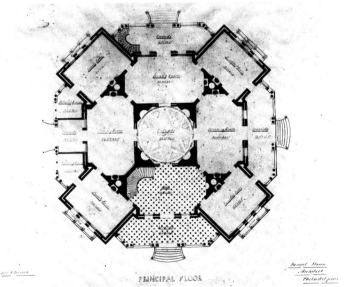

PRINCIPAL FLOOR

Elevation and plan of Longwood, Haller Nutt House, Natchez, Mississippi, drawn by
Samuel Sloan, 1860. *Pilgrimage Garden Club*

194

Longwood, view of portico columns.

now. . . . I think after this the Octagon will be the style. So you must get up some other [designs] on patterns of this style." Nutt then added, "Model them so as not to be so large or expensive." A tinner from Philadelphia was busy on the roof in August, and furniture had been ordered from Philadelphia.

But it was now seven months after the secession of Mississippi, hard feelings were mounting and there was danger that the Yankee workmen at Longwood might be attacked. In September, the tinner Walters and the last carpenter, Smith, returned hastily to the North. Only the basement rooms of Longwood would be completed—by plantation slaves in 1862. Though the interior of the upper stories has remained an empty shell, we can get some idea of Sloan's intentions for the interior from a description in his *Homestead Architecture*, published in 1861. A visitor would have crossed a front verandah, through an entrance hall, into an octagonal rotunda, twenty-four feet wide and three stories high, paved with encaustic tiles and ornamented with niches for statuary. When Nutt died in 1864, his fortunes had already been wrecked by the Civil War. Longwood is open to the public.

Haller Nutt enjoyed having his house become an object of curiosity and admiration among his neighbors. One of them, James Alexander Ventress of Woodville, a village south of Natchez, was one of that small but extraordinary group of planter-scholars who embellished Southern society.[47] About 1848 he married the niece of James L. Trask, a wealthy Massachusetts-born planter. In 1860, probably after meeting Sloan on one of his trips to Natchez, Ventress employed the architect to substantially rebuild the old Trask home at LaGrange plantation by adding a second story and a two-story Corinthian portico. Addison Hutton was sent to work at LaGrange between July and October, 1860, assisted by Joseph McIlwaine, a carpenter from Philadelphia. In late 1861, Sloan wrote that, because of the mounting sectional hostility, his workmen "have been drove from Col. Ventress's building . . . and they barely escaped with their lives."[48] The house at LaGrange burned in 1908, but some of the columns remain standing in splendid ruin.

LaGrange, James Alexander Ventress House, Woodville, Mississippi, as enlarged in 1860 by Samuel Sloan. *Private Collection*.

Longwood and LaGrange remind us how a closer look at Southern architecture reveals forgotten truths about Southern society. The South was an expanding frontier throughout the first half of the 19th century. Yankee merchants, Yankee builders and Yankee settlers flocked to the South in search of opportunity and provided the skills so necessary to create a new society in the Southern forests. The Civil War caused future Americans to forget, or deny, an invasion of Yankee talent and enthusiasm and decades of harmonious regional cooperation which created the society and architecture of the Old South.

Notes

The two most important sources of information about historic buildings in Mississippi and Alabama are the Mississippi Department of Archives and History, Historic Preservation Division, P.O. Box 571, Jackson, Mississippi 39205, and the Alabama Historical Commission, 725 Monroe Street, Montgomery, Alabama 36130. The following notes indicate, in place of a separate bibliography, useful manuscript and published sources. The notes also thank several local experts for their guidance and encouragement. Without the help of these works and generous friends a book like *Architecture of the Old South* would be impossible. The reader's attention is called to Robert Gamble, *The Alabama Catalogue . . . A Guide to the Early Architecture of the State* (University, Alabama, 1987), the best of the catalogues of Historic American Buildings Survey materials in the South.

I. COLONY AND FRONTIER

1. For more about colonial building in this area, see Samuel Wilson, Jr., *The Architecture of Colonial Louisiana* (Lafayette, La., 1987).

2. Phillip Pittman, *The Present State of the European Settlements on the Mississippi* [1770] (Cleveland, 1906).

3. Charles S. Davis, *The Cotton Kingdom in Alabama* (Montgomery, 1939), 16.

4. See Charles D. Lowery, "The Great Migration to the Mississippi Territory," *Journal of Mississippi History* (hereafter cited as *JMH*), XXX (1968), 173–192.

5. William Ely's letters appear in *The Alabama Review*, III (January, 1950).

6. Sarah Fountain's letters appear in Clement Eaton, *The Leaven of Democracy* (New York, 1963), 261.

7. "Autobiography of Gideon Lincecum," *Mississippi Historical Society Publications*, VIII (Oxford, 1904), 471.

8. Samuel S. Forman, *Narrative of a Journey down the Ohio and Mississippi in 1789–90* [1849] (Cincinnati, 1888), 53.

9. Clement Eaton, *op. cit.*, 262–263.

10. Philip Henry Gosse, *Letters from Alabama, Chiefly Relating to Natural History* (London, 1859), 151–155. Sentences from these pages have been abridged for convenient quotation.

11. Benjamin Smith, manuscript autobiography, c. 1921, Mississippi Department of Archives and History.

12. Harriet Martineau, *Society in America* (New York, 1837), I, 221.

13. Ltr. of Elizabeth Hathaway Larabee, July 8, 1842, Hathaway Family Papers, Cornell University.

14. Hope Summerell Chamberlain, *Old Days in Chapel Hill . . . Life and Letters of Cornelia Phillips Spencer* (Chapel Hill, 1926), 64–65. Sentences from these pages have been abridged for convenient quotation. I am indebted to Marshall Bullock of Chapel Hill for bringing this reference to my attention.

II. THE FEDERAL ERA

1. "Manuscript Journal of Geo. Hunter up the Red and Washita Rivers . . . 1804", typescript, Louisiana State University, 4–5.

2. Ltr. of Levi Weeks, October, 1812, Levi Weeks Papers, Mississippi Department of Archives and History.

3. Henry Hunt ltr., 1807, Sargent Papers, Massachusetts Historical Society.

4. Milly McGehee, "Auburn in Natchez," *Antiques* CXI (1977), 546–553.

5. Levi Weeks to Ep Hoyt, October 27, 1812, Weeks Papers, Mississippi Department of Archives and History.

6. This important document was presented, but misinterpreted, by Arthur H. DeRosier, Jr., "Carpenter's Estimate on the Building of 'The Forest'" in *JMH*, XXVII (1965), 259–264. The mistake was corrected by Alma Carpenter, "A Note on the History of the Forest Plantation," *JMH*, XLVI (1984), 130–137.

7. [Joseph Holt Ingraham], *The South-West by a Yankee* (New York, 1835), II, 81.

8. Samuel Wilson, Jr., "Clifton, An Ill-fated Natchez Mansion," *JMH*, XLVI (1984), 179–190.

9. William B. Bynum of the Historical Foundation of the Presbyterian and Reformed Churches, Montreat, N.C., suggests that the architect may have been Dr. Rush Nutt. See William B. Lowrance, *The Story of the Old Rodney Presbyterian Church* (Port Gibson, Ms., 1955).

10. Anne Newport Royall, *Letters from Alabama* [1818] (University, Al., 1969), 119.

11. Lucius Bierce, *Travels in the Southland* (Columbus, Oh., 1966), 96.

12. Harvie Jones, "Federal Period Residential Architecture in Huntsville and Madison County," *Historic Huntsville Quarterly*, VII (Fall, 1980). The author is indebted to Harvie Jones for encouragement and information.

13. Harvie Jones, "The Maria Howard Weeden House," *Historic Huntsville Quarterly*, VIII (Fall, 1981).

14. Sam Earle Hobbs, "History of Early Cahaba: Alabama's First State Capital," *Alabama Historical Quarterly* (hereafter cited as *AHQ*), XXXI (1969), 155–182.

15. Clement Eaton, *The Leaven of Democracy* (New York, 1963), 246–247.

16. Robert O. Mellown, "Alabama's Fourth Capitol: Construction of the State House in Tuscaloosa," *The Alabama Review*, XLI, No. 4 (October, 1987), 259–283.

17. *Alabama Intelligencer and States Rights Expositor*, Tuscaloosa, November 12, 1831.

18. *Southern Advocate*, Huntsville, October 9, 1830.

19. *The Democrat*, Huntsville, May 23, 1828.

III. THE GREEK REVIVAL

1. *Alabama Intelligencer and States Rights Expositor*, Tuscaloosa, April 20, 1831.

2. Contract between William Nichols and Ezra Williams, Mississippi Department of Archives and History.

3. Joseph G. Baldwin, *Flush Times of Alabama and Mississippi* (New York, 1853), 82–83.

4. Melissa P. Russell, diary, 1835, Alabama Department of Archives and History.

5. Arthur Scully, Jr., *James Dakin, Architect* (Baton Rouge, 1973) is the principal source for information on the Dakin brothers. James Gallier published an autobiography in Paris in 1864.

6. *Mississippi Free Trader*, Natchez, November 27, 1835.

7. The building committee exhibited plans and specifications at the office of Henry Tooley, "one of the building committee." *Daily Courier*, Natchez, May 31, 1833.

8. "Mr. Brown" advertised in the Natchez *Daily Courier*, November 25, 1837, that he had "several years of experience in New York and vicinity." He may have been the John C. Brown listed in 1830–31 New York City directories.

9. *Mississippi Free Trader and Natchez Gazette*, January 22, 1836.

10. The author is indebted to the files of Historic Natchez Foundation for information about Gemmell and other builders of this period in Natchez.

11. *Daily Courier*, Natchez, November 9, 1837.

12. *Weekly Courier and Journal*, Natchez, March 16, 1838.

13. *Alabama Intelligencer and States Rights Expositor*, Tuscaloosa, November 12, 1831.

14. In the October 2, 1835, issue of *The Mississippian*, Jackson, Lawrence announced he was "ready to furnish plans."

15. "Proceedings of the Board of Commissioners of Public Buildings in the State of Mississippi," I, 1836–41, Mississippi Department of Archives and History.

16. Quoted in C. Ford Peatross and Robert O. Mellown, *William Nichols, Architect* (Tuscaloosa, 1979), 29. I am most grateful to Robert Mellown, University of Alabama, whose accomplishments are equalled by his generosity, for information about William Nichols.

17. F. A. Stafford advertised in *The Mississippian*, Jackson, August 2, 1839.

18. *The Mississippian*, Jackson, August 16, 1839, cited in William D. McCain, *The Story of Jackson* (Jackson, 1953), I, 123.

19. See James Allen Cabaniss, *A History of the University of Mississippi* (Oxford, Ms., 1949).

20. John Fulton, *Memoirs of Frederick A. P. Barnard* (New York, 1896).

21. Robert O. Mellown and Gene Byrd, "F.A.P. Barnard and Alabama's First Observatory," *Journal of the Alabama Academy of Science*, LVII (January, 1986), 39–44.

22. Quoted in C. Ford Peatross and Robert O. Mellown, *op. cit.*, 29.

23. Linda Bayer, "George Steele, Huntsville's Antebellum Architect," *Historic Huntsville Quarterly*, V, No. 3 (Spring, 1979), 3–22.

24. *The Democrat*, Huntsville, October 8, 1834.

25. Patricia H. Ryan, *Cease Not to Think of Me: The Steele Family Letters* (Huntsville, 1979), 15.

26. *The Democrat*, Huntsville, September 9, 1835.

27. *The Democrat*, Huntsville, September 16, 1835.

28. *The Democrat*, Huntsville, November 15, 1836.

29. *The Democrat*, Huntsville, March 17, 1838.

30. Steele served as a member of one of the building committees for the 1846 Capitol at Montgomery.

31. *Limestone News*, Athens, August 10, 1859.

32. Richard J. Webster, "Stephen D. Button, Italianate Stylist," M.A. thesis, University of Delaware, 1963.

33. W. G. Button wrote Thomas M. Owen, August 3, 1918: "My father, I have always heard, spent five years in the South, New Orleans, Mobile, Montgomery, and Florida." Alabama Department of Archives and History.

34. Joseph E. King to Alice Tompkins, June 4, 1848, Duke University Library.

35. A. J. Downing to Charles Crommelin, March 9, 1846: "He [Gill] stuccoed the exterior of my own house." Alabama Department of Archives and History.

36. *The Democrat*, Huntsville, November 24, 1847.

37. *Daily Alabama Journal*, Montgomery, March 12, 1850.

38. Nimrod E. Benson to Gov. Collier, March 13, 1850: "Mr. Pratt today submitted a plan for the new State House . . . of the Doric order." Alabama Department of Archives and History.

39. S.F.H. Tarrant, *Hon. Daniel Pratt* (Richmond, 1904), 63.

40. Donna C. Hole, "Daniel Pratt and Barachias Holt: Architects of the Alabama State Capitol," *Alabama Review*, XXXVII (1984), 83–97.

41. The author is indebted to Mary Ann Neely, of Montgomery's Landmarks Foundation, for information about Figh.

42. Benjamin Parsons to Richard Upjohn, November 27, 1854, November 29, 1854, Upjohn Papers, New York Public Library.

43. "Report of the Commissioners of the Lunatic Asylum," January 1, 1852, typescript, Mississippi Department of Archives and History.

44. "James Junior: A Remarkable Man and His Mansions," *The Commercial Appeal*, Memphis, April 23, 1978.

45. Patrick Murphy, Diary, May 16, 1856, Murphy Papers, Louisiana State University. "Willis withdrew or gave up the job. Tom [Weldon] thinks he will get it."

46. Gordon A. Cotton, *The Old Court House* (Vicksburg, 1982).

47. *Courier*, Natchez, May 31, 1883.

48. *Mississippi Free Trader*, Natchez, February 19, 1836. William Fox and Company, Natchez booksellers, offered Peter Nicholson's *The Mechanic's Companion* (New York, 1831) in 1833. *Natchez Courier and Adams, Jefferson and Franklin Advertiser*, February 15, 1833.

49. The author is indebted to Mrs. Helen Crawford of Hamilton, Mississippi, for information about Aberdeen.

50. Walter S. Patton, J. Glenn Little and Luther Hill, "General Nathan Bryan Whitfield and Gaineswood," typescript, Alabama Historical Commission, 1972.

51. Nathan B. Whitfield to Needham Bryan Whitfield, February 29, 1848, private collection. I am indebted to Bryan W. Whitfield, Jr., of Brookside, Kentucky, for copies of this and other letters.

52. Whitfield to Cousin Rachel, February, 1848, quoted in Patton, Little and Hull, *op. cit.*, 22.

53. Whitfield to Needham Whitfield, March 21, 1848, private collection.

54. Whitfield to Bryan Whitfield, October, 1848, quoted in Patton, Little and Hull, *op. cit.*, 23.

55. Whitfield to "my dear Daughter," February 13, 1859, private collection.

56. Whitfield to Cousin Rachel, 1861, quoted in Patton, Little and Hill, *op. cit.*, 29–30.

57. Albert Diettel, Notebook, Michael D. Wynne Collection, Louisiana State University. Obituary appeared in *Daily Picayune*, New Orleans, October 11, 1896.

58. Henry Howard's autobiography was published in a c. 1950 exhibition catalogue, a copy of which is located at the Tulane University Library. Henry Howard's obituary appeared in the *Times-Democrat*, New Orleans, November 26, 1884.

59. The author is indebted to Kenneth H. P'Pool, who generously allowed me to read and enjoy his unpublished "Columbus, Mississippi: An Architectural History, 1817–1866," typescript.

IV. ROMANTIC STYLES

1. *The Daily Democrat*, Natchez, September 11, 1889.

2. Joseph Holt Ingraham recounts much of his biography in his book, *The South-West by a Yankee* (New York, 1835).

3. James Lundy Sykes, *A History of St. John's Parish* (n.p., n.d.).

4. *The Southern Advocate*, Huntsville, June 28, 1854 and June 30, 1854.

5. John C. Frank, "Adolphus Heiman, Architect and Soldier," *Tennessee Historical Quarterly*, V, 35–57.

6. Frank Wills, *Ancient English Ecclesiastical Architecture* (New York, 1850), 84, 88.

7. Elizabeth Claire Welch, "Ecclesiology: Its Influence on the Gothic Revival in Antebellum Mississippi," M.A. thesis, University of Virginia, 1981.

8. Elizabeth Larabee to her "Dear Sister," January 15, 1854, Hathaway Family Papers, Cornell University.

9. Walter C. Whitaker, *History of the Protestant Episcopal Church in Alabama* (Birmingham, 1898).

10. May Averil Cook, *Historical St. John's Church* (Montgomery, 1936).

11. *Weekly Alabama Journal*, Montgomery, May 26, 1855.

12. George Cushman to Richard Upjohn, Upjohn Papers, New York Public Library, August 5, 1855.

13. Thomas B. Bailey to Richard Upjohn, October 26, 1855, Upjohn Papers, New York Public Library.

14. David Kerr to Richard Upjohn, May 4, 1847; M. J. Conley to Upjohn, December 6, 1858; Upjohn Papers, New York Public Library.

15. Lucy Green Nelson, *St. John's Church, Mobile, A. History* (Mobile, 1963).

16. *Dallas Gazette*, Selma, March 31, 1854.

17. William M. Spencer, "St. Andrew's Church, Prairieville," *The Alabama Review*, XIV (1961), 18–30.

18. Alan Smith Thompson, "Gothic Revival Architecture in Ante-Bellum Alabama," M.A. thesis, University of Alabama, 1963.

19. David Weir to A. J. Davis, December 10, 1855, Davis Collection, Avery Architectural and Fine Arts Library; A. J. Davis, Diary, Metropolitan Museum of Art, New York; in the diary, December 10, 26–27, 1855, p. 181, Davis states, "Made sketch plans for house like Brown's Rahway for Andrew Weir of Norfolk."

20. J. H. de Bose to Richard Upjohn, April 3, 1851, Upjohn Papers, New York Public Library, Astor, Lenox and Tilden Foundations.

21. L. N. Walthall to Richard Upjohn, January 6, 1854, Upjohn Papers, New York Public Library.

22. Walthall to Upjohn, January 31, 1854, Upjohn Papers, New York Public Library.

23. Walthall to Upjohn, October 22, 1857, Upjohn Papers, New York Public Library.

24. William Hart to Upjohn, May 9, 1858, Upjohn Papers, New York Public Library.

25. Hart to Upjohn, [September, 1858], Upjohn Papers, New York Public Library.

26. Receipt, Alexander T. Stewart and Company, New York, to E. K. Carlisle, September, 1860, Carlisle Papers, Alabama Department of Archives and History.

27. *Limestone News*, Athens, August 10, 1859. Italics added for emphasis.

28. "Specifications of Grace Church at Canton," March 12, 1853, photocopy at Mississippi Department of Archives and History, names Larmour as builder of the church and parsonage.

29. *The American Citizen*, Canton, November 26, 1853.

30. *The American Citizen*, Canton, June 10, 1854. Another designer, carver, builder and architect of interest was English-born B. C. Gough, who, in 1857, offered to draw plans, perspective views, cast plaster mouldings and centerpieces and plaster ornaments, also design cottages, villas and mansions in different orders and styles and teach stairbuilding to other builders. *The American Citizen*, Canton, October 1, 1857, July 31, 1856.

31. Henry Sansom to Miss Hathaway, September 30, 1857, Hathaway Family Papers, Cornell University Library.

32. *Daily Courier*, Natchez, February 4, 1853.

33. See *Illustrations of Iron Architecture Made by the Architectural Iron Works of the City of New York* (New York, 1865).

34. *Weekly Alabama Journal*, Montgomery, April 29, 1854.

35. Robert O. Mellown, "The Construction of the Alabama Insane Hospital, 1852–1861," *Alabama Review*, XXXVIII (1985), 83–104.

36. Thomas Kirkbride, *On the Construction, Organization, and General Arrangements of Hospitals for the Insane* (Philadelphia, 1854).

37. *Annual Report of the Officers of the Alabama Insane Hospital at Tuscaloosa for the Year 1861* (Montgomery, 1861).

38. Anderson has not been identified. A Philadelphia city directory of the period lists "Alexander Anderson, marble polisher."

39. Robert Jemison to John Stewart, April 29, 1860, Letterbook 141, 78–83, and December 31, 1859, Letterbrook 710, both in Jemison Papers, University of Alabama.

40. *Weekly Alabama Journal*, Montgomery, March 11, 1854. The author is again indebted to Robert O. Mellown, University of Alabama, for information about Sloan and Stewart. He generously shared material that will soon be published in an article tentatively entitled "Philadelphia Architects in Dixie, Deep South Commissions by Sloan and Stewart."

41. Rhoda Coleman Ellison, *History of Huntingdon College, 1854–1954* (University, Al., 1954), 9. See *Macon Republican*, Tuskegee, February 21, 1865.

42. Contract, January, 1860, Jemison Papers, University of Alabama.

43. Lewis remains unidentified. Philadelphia directories of the period list many carpenters with that last name.

44. Robert Jemison to John Steward, August 29, 1859, Letterbook 141, 628–629, Jemison Papers, University of Alabama.

45. Documents relating to the construction of Longwood, including the letters quoted below, are at the Huntington Library and Duke University. The best of them are published in Ina May Ogletree McAdams, *The Building of Longwood* (Austin, Tx., 1972).

46. Elizabeth Biddle Yarnall, *Addison Hutton* (Philadelphia, 1974).

47. The author is indebted to Lynda L. Crist, Rice University, for information about Ventress and LaGrange. See Linda Lasswell Crist, "Useful in His Day and Generation: James Alexander Ventress," Ph.D. dissertation, University of Tennessee, 1980. See also James A. Ventress Family Papers, Mississippi Department of Archives and History.

48. Quoted in McAdams, *op. cit.*, 83.

Index